Skills of the Assassin

Understanding the Tactics of The Professional Killer

R.J. GODLEWSKI

TACTICAL EXTRACTIONS

THREAT RESOLUTION SERVICES

Title page and chapter conclusion image: © deaff - Fotolia.com

Title page illustration: © Tactical Extractions.

Published by CreateSpace Independent Publishing Platform.

ISBN: 1480240001
ISBN-13: 978-1480240001

Warning: All individual combat and personal survival activities involve risk or injury, to oneself and to others, and great care must be exercised in carrying out any such activities. Expert legal and technical guidance should be consulted and equipment checked for reliability before any activities described within this book are carried out. The publisher, the author, or any affiliated party cannot assume responsibility for damage to property or injury, death or loss to persons that may result from carrying out the activities described within this book. In carrying out such activities described within this book, persons do so entirely at their own risk..

DEDICATION

To all who devote his or her life to defeating evil, wherever it may be found, and protecting innocent human lives wherever they may live.

CONTENTS

ACKNOWLEDGMENTS

To God the Father, the Son, and the Holy Spirit, without Whom I would find no talent, no opportunity, and no friends with which to affect either my trade or my interests.

Deo gratias.

And to the extraordinary individuals who have taught me well (or lent me considerable advice and knowledge) over the past half-century.

Muchas gracias a mis amigos secretos...

1

WHY A BOOK ON THE SKILLS OF AN ASSASSIN?

Libraries are filled with books on *the* Assassins, their history, exploits, and even modern video gamers' infatuation with the ancient cult. However, there remains little discussed on the particular skill sets of *an* assassin – the modern terrorist, hired killer, or transnational criminal that *you* are most likely to encounter within the early decades of the 21st century. Maces, swords and other archaic devices of war are not applicable for today's deadly environment. The modern assassin may strike with sabot rounds in his or her rifle so as to confuse or divert police CSI units. Alternatively, an "old school" assassin may choose to mix two drops of liquid Temik equally with dimethylsulfoxide onto an executive's briefcase. Perhaps, even, the distant assassin may ultimately hack into a hospital's computerized records to manipulate a patient's prescription drug order to render a lethal dose. Three methods, one result: a dead human

1

being and an untraceable villain.

Given that comparatively few in the world today find the need – or stomach – to delve into the depravity of intentionally killing another individual, consideration of the tools and techniques of the trade largely remain outside the discussion of civilized society. And for good reason; people who learn about computers, for instance, actually *intend* to use them at some point in time. Is there *anyone* out there who needs to study the tactics and techniques of intentional killing that **does** not intend to employ them? Yes, of course. Military, law enforcement, security personnel and concerned citizens *all* possess an inherent need for understanding threats, including terroristic, political, and criminal assassination. After all, thousands – if not millions – of people have investigated the assassination of President John F. Kennedy to varying degrees and they all cannot be planning the murder of a national leader.

Life remains serious business, despite that most people go through it indifferent to the many obstacles and menaces that serve to shorten their presence here on earth. Conscientious people, for instance, may study about their motor vehicle before using it, read their computer manual before voyaging online, or even enrolling within a cooking class prior to inviting that special someone over for dinner. Therefore, it remains prudent for the security-conscious individual to understand the threats that he or she encounters, despite the rarity of the event.

So, Just Who Are Today's Assassins?

In Hollywood, your typical "assassin" represents a breathtakingly beautiful woman or, perhaps, a beefed-up hunk with just enough facial hair to drive women crazy. This violates the first law of covert warfare: do *not* call unnecessary attention to yourself. A five-foot-nine blond sashaying down the boulevard in stiletto heels is going to attract as much attention from men as a six-foot-four Chippendale's dancer driving an Audi A8 W12 in the fast lane will from women. A good assassin may very well represent someone who had been living next door to you for forty years and drives your children to school on odd days of the week. He or she may also represent your slightly-off sibling that never seems to hold a steady job and, yet, excels at a position that would end your life before you even answered the wanted ads – assuming that such positions could even be mentioned within the periodicals.

In fact, an assassin may hail from virtually any location, any background, and exhibit any appearance imaginable, which makes them decidedly difficult to describe physically. Moreover, assassins neither apply nor recruit. They are eternally "there" and those who have need of hiring them possess their own *unique* ways for locating them. For the sake of discussion, we shall categorize the breed into one of the following groups:

- **Nation-state actors** who operate at the behest of their governments and conduct operations against rival military, terrorist/criminal, and governmental targets;

- **Non-state actors** who operate under the auspices, or for the benefit, of an organizational client such as a terrorist organization, transnational criminal organization, or perhaps an illicit business or political enterprise;

- **Lone wolf** assassins who work for any of the above or an individual client as a standalone asset.

This book will concentrate on the latter, as individual assassins represent the most diabolical of the species and, perhaps, the least understood. Both nation-state and non-state actors serve as a function of the broader body politic and, therefore, adhere to some form of discretion no matter how sinister that may be. The stereotypical "lone assassin", contrarily, may serve an individual with little more than a personal grudge against another. That is, the entire course of human history may change drastically upon the chance employment of even a "lucky" assailant. One only needs to conduct a short study of history in order to validate this argument.

To remain successful within his or her endeavors, assassins must adhere to the following personal characteristics.[1]

> ✓ Dedication towards purpose of mission.
>
> ✓ Physical, mental, and emotional strength.
>
> ✓ Outstanding knowledge of weapons and the technology of death.
>
> ✓ Possess high security awareness.
>
> ✓ Personal intelligence and ability to transit operational areas.
>
> ✓ Perseverance for survival.

These, of course, represent the requirements for a professional assassin, not one employed within a *lost assassination* where the perpetrator becomes expendable and therefore expected to die or be captured. In this latter case, fanatics, mentally unstable, and other questionable characters remain the norm and not the exception. They are usually employed to affect history without drawing unnecessary attention to sponsoring bodies. However, we will not discuss

---

[1] Culled from various versions of the "CIA Assassination Manual" produced during the 1950s.

these "one-off" individuals for their role borders upon suicidal or kamikaze missions ill-suited for the emotionless, calculating, dedicated, and persistent professional.

Why Do Assassins Exist?

This represents, perhaps, the most honest question regarding the subject and, very likely, the one that cannot ever be answered to the satisfaction of everyone. The short answer is, of course, that people resort to violence to affect their grievances. A business executive may seek to eliminate the key scientist behind a competitor's profitable development. An Islamist terrorist may seek to remove a moderate imam speaking out against the travesties of radicalism. The long answer remains a bit more chilling and requires significant study, far beyond the limitations of this book. Assassins exist because certain individuals and governments operate outside the confines of domestic and international law. That is, these entities have determined that selected individuals should perish rather than remain a potential threat to their ambitions.

During periods of war, "targeted killings" generally do not qualify as assassinations.[2] For the most part, however, such actions are avoided lest the military find itself charged with conducting paramilitary death squads applying extrajudicial execution.[3]This remains fully understandable; militaries are governed by a nation's leadership and, whether democracy or despot, public officials tend to shy away from notoriety (which explains why most hardcore despots eliminate the free press when they take over). Corrupt individuals and organizations, to the contrary, generally operate outside the care of the national media and, employing *professional* killers, bear the capability

---

[2] Thomas B. Hunter, *Targeted Killing: Self-Defense, Preemption, and the War on Terrorism* (Lexington, KY: BookSurge, 5-7.

[3] Michael L. Gross, *Moral Dilemmas of Modern War: Torture, Assassination, and Blackmail in an Age of Asymmetric Conflict* (New York: Cambridge University Press, 2010), 101.

of taking out targets outside of such public, legal consideration.

It represents this fundamental quality – to kill without attracting attention – that permits professional assassins to flourish within the modern world as they have throughout human history. Hollywood, in the best traditions of fantasy, always exacerbates the field leading to such ridiculous methods of attack that one wonders how, precisely, the assassin could conceivably get away with the crime. One notable exception, particularly for its depiction of an authentic urban guerrilla sniping environment, remains 1973's *The Day of the Jackal,* based upon the novel by Frederick Forsyth.[4]

In reality, assassins represent a traditional contractual relationship whereby the assassin offers a particular service – the elimination of a specific target without the client becoming exposed to the event. If the job could be bungled, then *anyone* could fill the role. The same holds true with neurosurgeons and diamond cutters.

The Need to Study Assassins and Their Trade.

As with criminology and terrorism research, the astute analyst and defender *must* acquire broad knowledge of his or her quarry. Assassins, though operating within relative rarity amongst the world's population, do nevertheless exist. They confound law enforcement agencies, military officers, and, often, political leaders. Far too often, academic and popular studies confront the legalities and morality of the field as if assassins themselves consult political polls before they affect their deadly trade. As a result, few bother to study the techniques and tools of this trade from the purely

---

[4] John West, *Fry the Brain: The Art of Urban Sniping and It's Role in Modern Guerrilla Warfare* (Countryside, VA: SSI, 2008), 87; *The Day of the Jackal* DVD (Universal Home Videos, 1998).

informational perspective.

Inasmuch as the media generally defines any long-range shooter as a "sniper", many people erroneously conclude that any killer or attempted killer of a publicly recognized figure constitutes an authentic assassin. This represents a false appreciation of an individual's talents. Mark David Chapman did not "assassinate" singer John Lennon anymore than John Hinckley, Jr. attempted to assassinate President Ronald Reagan. Both men simply represented intentional murderers, one successful and the other not. Neither sought more than the public or personal glory that came with his crime. Again, this diverts from the fundamental law of working as a professional killer: avoiding notoriety from the action. Consider, for instance, how successful a bank robber could be if it remained public knowledge that he or she enjoyed stealing people's life savings? Could that individual possibly walk into any bank and be served with courtesy and trust? Of course not. Only the Keystone Kops sought villains in striped uniforms.

Because assassins are virtually impossible to describe, the task then shifts to understanding their techniques. Again, this remains nearly impossible to discuss for each individual possesses a certain *modus operandi* in the form of his or her basic knowledge. No assassins *ever* employ the same technique or tactic, but each bears a certain fundamental base of knowledge. Just as with any carpenter, welder, or even physician. Woodworkers, for instance, may elect to build with power or hand tools, but the function of each instrument remains the same whether you are using electricity or muscles to bore a hole through a two-inch oak plank.

An assassin, much like a telegraph operator, bears a certain style that may or may not be detected by those familiar with his trade. In fact, every tradesperson does bear that unique *modus operandi* no matter how faint or obscure. For this

7

reason alone, perhaps, there remains a need to study the tactics and skill sets of independent, professional killers. Hence, the need for a book on this most obscure of individuals. From a careful study of the mentality, physical conditioning and disguise, weapons familiarization and smuggling, international business and money laundering, safe havens and avenues of escape of the trade, as well as an examination of death and how it occurs, we can perceive events not yet actualized. Through this book, it is hoped that the reader will emerge within a better position to understand professional assassination devoid of the hysterics and fantasy imposed by Hollywood and the press.

2

A NEIGHBOR WITH A PENCHANT FOR DEATH: THE MENTALITY OF AN ASSASSIN.

There remain four fundamental types of human individuals worth discussing within this book. The first group cannot kill another human being no matter what the provocation. The second kills mercilessly with little motivation. The third group, while they can be trained to kill, will not normally do so unless they perceive a grave threat to themselves or some other individual under their care. The fourth and final group represents those rare individuals that can kill and kill repeatedly and yet restrict their killing to a rather well defined parameter. Professional soldiers (comprising neither conscripts nor volunteer enlistees) and assassins fall into this final group.

This does not mean that either professional soldiers (e.g., the traditional mercenary) or assassins represent fanatical killing machines. For instance, a professional soldier may find employment only a few months out of the year (situations such as Afghanistan and Iraq excepted) and then encounter only a few combat situations over the course of many contracts. The assassin, to the contrary, may have to travel continuously around the world and then only find one "opportunity" per year. This may seem a low number, considering that the United States alone witnesses some 6,000 unsolved murders each year, but the inability to solve a particular case does not automatically endorse the exploits of a professional killer.[5]

Contrary to popular opinion, most crimes – of whatever persuasion – seldom reach the solved status. In today's age of CSI-type television shows that need to solve the most complex (and, therefore, *entertaining*) crimes within a sixty-minute broadcast, most agencies remain sufficiently understaffed and under budget to achieve the degree of success that Hollywood purports. Added to this problem remains the number of murders that take place amongst rural environments or amongst populations that escape the attention of resource limited police departments (i.e., drug users, prostitutes, the homeless, etc.). Finally, few individuals remain receptive to testifying within the trial of a vicious murderer or criminal.

All these factors reduce the potential that any one assassin will remain gainfully employed until retirement age. Therefore, a professional assassin remains unlikely to reach that phase of desensitization that breeds fanatical killers. In fact, for the U.S. government to develop military assassins (ostensibly those employed to kill key enemy personnel), required an elaborate psychological program based upon classical conditioning and social learning methodologies.[6] What this means is that if the U.S. government, with its vast resources and virtually

---

[5] http://www.timesrecordnews.com/news/2010/may/24/unsolved-homicides/ Accessed November 2012.

[6] Dave Grossman, *On Killing: The Psychological Cost of Learning to Kill in War and Society* (New York: Back Bay Books, 2009), 310-311.

unlimited funds (if not morals) bears great difficulty in turning out professional killers, then *true* assassins remain remarkably rarer still. What is left within the world remains institutionalized killers populating street gangs, drug cartels, terrorist organizations and mafia crime families. These, however, represent individuals protected more by the "institution" than personal ability.

Individual assassins, to the contrary, fall outside group protection and therefore must operate *within* society – not external to it – in order to avoid apprehension by law enforcement or retaliation from any parties protecting the target. The true professional assassin of the modern era bears traits developed over centuries of primal human interaction.

Your Neighbor, The Suitcase Ninja.

Humans have largely lost their fundamental ability to survive within the wild. More than anything else, this prevents them from functioning within society as a whole.[7] An assassin, however, must blend in with varying cultures, maintain awareness of any and all threats (including, especially, being apprehended by indigenous law enforcement authorities), and follow their quarry surreptitiously through the streets of the planet's most populous cities or along country roads lined with cornfields and grazing cattle. This highly successful individual swears by the "way of invisibility" and incorporates the ability to move as if a phantom, develop covert reconnaissance techniques, blend in with the night at every opportunity, distract the victim's attention, and master practical and effective disguise.[8] In other words, the modern professional killer channels the very soul of the ancient ninja warrior.

---

[7] Nearly every individual on the planet gravitates towards like-minded groups and associations.

[8] Stephen K. Hayes, *The Ninja and Their Secret Fighting Art* (Rutland, VT: Charles E. Tuttle Company, 1981), 98-114.

The ancient Japanese killers did not grimace over what it took to terminate their prey. Unlike the samurai, who lived by a well-defined code of existence, the ninja simply perfected their trade. Today, their memory remains tarnished by those, such as Hollywood, who sensationalize their antics or fictionalize their abilities. Yes, ninja could scale vertical walls. So, too, can any well-equipped carpenter. Yes, ninja could disappear into the night without leaving any trace of their arrival. So, too, can any well-trained deer hunter. Yes, ninja could unnerve even the most stoical citizen upon mere word of their presence. So, too, can any well-experienced criminal investigator.

None of these traits represents anything particularly noteworthy. What makes such feats "extraordinary" remains that most individuals alive today have consciously abandoned the abilities bestowed upon human beings through countless eons of evolutionary development. Humans generally do not pay much attention to their own lives, let alone the broader world around them. The prevalence of magicians underscores this, as there remains nothing inherently "magical" about their trade. People are routinely deceived because they *can* be deceived. An assassin intimately understands this and therefore he or she remains the most powerful deceiver of all. In the words of one of the best deceivers of all time, it takes practice to tell a convincing lie and even greater practice to *live* such a convincing lie.[9]

The assassin bears this ability to "live a convincing lie" simply because he or she offers a profound disconnect with people in general and society in particular. This disconnect does not mean the same thing as representing a social outcast or recluse. On the contrary. The professional assassin *cannot* avoid association or intermingling with people. The difference,

---

[9] H. Keith Melton and Robert Wallace, *The C.I.A. Manual of Trickery and Deception* (New York: Harper Collins/William Morrow, 2009), 69.

however, is that he or she employs these socializations as a mere "tool" in order to more effectively carry out their devious trade.

Social Skills of the Assassin.

Inasmuch as an experienced author can keep several literary projects ongoing at any one time – and maintain the ability to delve into each project quite at random without losing track of where the storyline rests – a professional killer remains equally adept at compartmentalizing his activities. Whereas some, perhaps, might offer an example of bipolar disorder, the assassin simply remains skilled at *presence*. This cyclic perception of location, time, and situation remains difficult for most, but for the professional killer understanding the intimate dynamics of where he or she is located at any particular time and what they are supposed to be doing at that precise moment rests as a fundamental condition of employment.

Few other individuals can, for instance, maintain a home as a typical suburbanite, identify which Armani suit to wear at a million dollar fundraiser, *and* understand a thousand different ways in which an individual may die without a medical examiner becoming suspicious over their death. Alternatively, the assassin may understand how to drive a tractor-trailer rig, fly a Gulfstream corporate jet, or relate to the intrinsic nature of diamond cutting as may be required. This does *not* suggest that the assassin may be able to *carry out* these diverse functions. Rather he or she may have to assume the role of trucker, pilot, or gemcutter in order to transit, loiter within, or approach a particular group.

These attributes fall squarely into the assassin's "*It is better to know 60% of a hundred different things than 100% of one.*"[10]

---

[10] Memorandum for the record, R.J. Godlewski's personal motto borrowed for effect.

Because of the comparative rarity of professional hits, this philosophy represents basic common sense. First, targeted victims generally do not come within the same trade and, secondly, any congregation of similar victims represents the possibility of the killer being isolated through repetition. All humans develop a set pattern, even if only subconsciously, and professional assassins remain no different. Targeting disparate victims is not only expected, it serves to prevent the professional from falling into a predictable trap. Other "creative" disciplines such as photography, music, writing, etc. sacrifice the artist's identity through style.

For obvious reasons, the assassin spends a great deal of time frequenting public places such as shopping malls, bars, and sporting events. Anywhere where people of all classes congregate and he or she can observe them and learn to emulate their peculiarities. An assassin, therefore, must not only learn how to act in public, they must understand *who* wears specific articles of clothing, *what* manners of speech a particular individual employs, and even *how* a normal individual acts under duress, injury, illness or insult.

Few people adequately understand how he or she is supposed to act, but the professional killer must intuitively understand how any number of people may behave, keeping this catalog file of cultures, classes, and characters locked away within his or her mind for instant retrieval should the need arise. Think about this for a moment. How many Hollywood actors have you watched perform on television or in the movies that bear the same character despite the magnitude of their roles? In fact, when we find an actor whose capabilities disguise their hackneyed identity, they are usually elevated amongst the greatest performers in theater history.

The "Knowledge Curator" That Kills for a Living.

Professional assassins, again, represent some of the most

intelligent and literate individuals living today. They bear more knowledge about human behavior than your typical psychologist, understand more about business than your typical executive, and accommodate more diverse physical activities than your typical athlete. They consume knowledge in the same manner as you breathe or sleep. When they wade through the sea of humanity, they absorb its peculiarities and lessons as if a sponge.

This does not represent a trivial trait, for they not only "hear all, see all, and know all", they *understand* all as well. This remains a characteristic sorely lacking within modern society as academics, politicians, and entertainers dilute the concept of intelligence. We can discuss this problem through two broad distinctions of such individual 'intelligence'.

- British theoretical physicist Stephen Hawking is widely hailed as the smartest living person alive. Yet, despite the power of his brain, it cannot permit him to walk, shake hands, or even eat like the rest of humanity;

- A recent television commercial for the impotency drug Viagra® showed several men sitting around a Nashville, Tennessee recording studio singing *Viva Viagra!* leaving astute viewers wondering how great the drug could be if they were *there* at 2 A.M. instead of at home in bed with their wives.

These examples place "intelligence" (that is, mental capability) into proper perspective. In the first case, how well could Stephen Hawking formulate new theories of the universe if his mind soared around the myriad of passionate thoughts that everyone else contends with on a daily basis? In the second case, what was the advertising agency thinking of when they were promoting the lovemaking ability of Viagra®? Both cases simply defeat popular expectations (if not recognition) through common sense. In this view, Stephen Hawking remains brilliant, but not spectacular and the drug advertisement perhaps spectacular, but not necessarily brilliant. A professional assassin must understand the intrinsic nature of this argument in order to survive.

That is, the professional must always scrutinize every thought and interaction to ascertain true intent of the individual or information available (this will be discussed in detail when we turn to matters of Intelligence as a discipline). For now, the aforementioned examples of Mr. Hawking and the Viagra® ad merely serve as instances where the "average" person would fall into line with conventional thought.

The assassin, to the contrary, cannot be led astray from raw emotions (e.g., the intelligence of a particular individual or the value of any pharmaceutical). *Everything* must be challenged, deciphered, and rationalized. Only then can the professional killer adequately accept a contract and efficiently carry out the deadly task. Ordinary people do not focus upon such discriminating factors and, in all likelihood, still would not understand why the two examples mentioned above were singled out.

The more an individual learns and remembers, the more he or she is likely to draw upon this knowledge to handle future challenges. For the assassin, even the most obscure thought or experience becomes a force-multiplier to affect their trade. A lesson they learned from, say, handling logistics for a previous contract may benefit him in preparing a future disguise as a freight forwarder. Or, perhaps, another assassin learned how to act like a hair stylist while she was simply having her hair done. Like the proverbial elephant, an astute assassin *never forgets anything,* no matter how seemingly inconsequential.

Decompression.

One trait that *all* assassins share remains a technique for dealing with the aftermath of killing another individual. Often, following ancient conflicts that necessarily involved close quarters combat, armies segregated their soldiers from the civilian population for several days in order to permit warriors to psychologically stand down from such brutal activities. These measures included isolation, cleaning weapons, what we would refer to today as "debriefing", and other measures designed to reduce the stress of taking human lives before the next episode of combat took place.

Assassins bear an even stronger challenge: they likely remain the only ones that know *why* they must recover psychologically. There remains no such thing as Assassins Anonymous where a professional killer can learn about meetings within the local newspaper. Instead, he or she must deal with the aftereffects of their trade personally and without arousing suspicion from anyone else. Remember, only psychopaths and drug-intoxicated killers remain completely remorseless. The assassin may ultimately consider *why* their victim warranted death – even if only in passing. This remains because the killing of non-combatants remains intensely traumatic and provides the assassin with limited motivation to kill the selected target, as it saps his or her ability to dehumanize the target (as, say, would soldiers of an army or even jihadists).[11]

In Hollywood, the avenues of release are simple: sex, booze, and tearing up the town. Unfortunately, even "biographies" from Hollywood remain sheer fantasy. The professional killer cannot expose him or herself to indiscretion and therefore sex, drinking, and drawing attention to oneself through raucous merrymaking are good for entertainment purposes, but little more. *Any* gesture to outside parties increases the assassin's threat from exposure. So how, exactly, does your typical

---

[11] Grossman, *On Killing*, 203.

professional killer calm down after a successful (or unsuccessful, for that matter) hit?

Pretty much like all *professional* people; assassins embark upon a number of crafts and hobbies. This may seem a bit trite to the uninitiated, but people with controlled (though not necessarily *controlling*) lifestyles need hobbies that emulate controlled environments. That is, anyone with a meticulous trade finds release within structured and ordered pastimes such as, say, painting, music, collecting, and even gardening. These activities permit individuals to build within a measured environment whether that involves assembling a stamp collection, growing an herbal garden, or simply stockpiling jazz records. As with knowledge, the individual simply does not horde. They *collect* discriminatingly.

3

NOW YOU SEE DEATH, NOW YOU DON'T: PHYSICAL CONDITIONING AND DISGUISE.

Few professional killers can survive very long within society who do not possess the stamina to endure long encounters with physical activity or maintain the capability of disappearing literally in plain sight of others. Both of these conditions warrant physical appearance, but an ability to disguise oneself forfeits all opportunity to "beef up" as would be the case with most athletes, body builders, and "Gym Queens". In some environments, muscle toning remains a dead giveaway of Western origins.

As with most fascinations within Western society, good intentions are often cast aside for unrealistic expectations. Henceforth, the aforementioned five-foot-nine blond in stilettos. Most women throughout the world remain decidedly shorter.[12]That *natural* blonds account for less than 2% of the global population further alienates the Hollywood vixen with a gun. In fact, the *only* advantage of being fair-haired remains the unique ability to accept almost any hair coloring imaginable, which, obviously, improves one's chances of employing effective disguises.

Nevertheless, even semi-permanent coloring can remain a liability for the assassin never reaches 'safe mode' even within their native setting. Inasmuch as physical condition is tailored towards toning more than 'beefing up', disguises revolve around practicality more than extraordinary. Because of this, a professional assassin's appearance must *always* be fluid. For instance, an astute professional understands that people, in general, do not retain sufficient concentration of memory to remember the face and appearance of an individual that they had just, moments before, asked directions from.

This provides an opportunity for the professional to employ "quick change" disguises that remain more practical than the ones described in movies or television. Among these include:

- A simple change of eyeglasses (far more noticeable than, say, eye color) can disrupt a citizen's ability to identify a particular individual. A mere shift from wire-frame eyeglasses to plastic frame eyeglasses allows a person to escape the "programmed memory" of an observer without actually leaving the presence of their gaze.[13]

- An man with a thin, graying mustache can darken his facial hair significantly with black mascara brushed in with a toothbrush, providing the 'look' of a healthy, *thick* moustache. To 'remove' the moustache (the

---

[12] http://www.disabled-world.com/artman/publish/height-chart.shtml. Accessed November, 2012.

[13] Memorandum for the record, R.J. Godlewski.

original, gray version being quite unnoticeable), all the professional needs to do is wipe his face with a wet handkerchief. Note: This option represents a one-way action, as enhancing the moustache requires far more time and effort than simply washing it away.

In either of the above situations, an individual can round a corner and reemerge as a completely different personality with little of any effort, though sufficient enough to confuse all but the most dedicated human tracker. Accordingly, the astute professional need not develop his craft as effectively as his trade is benefitted from a lazy population. Lack of attention from the public remains a clandestine operator's greatest force-multiplier.

Body by Assassin.

Bulked physiques remain quite impractical for any activity beyond, perhaps, photographic sessions. This remains because issues of *Sports Illustrated* or the latest *Victoria's Secret* catalog are designed to attract attention, not prevent it. No person wants to peruse a sports magazine with scrawny middle school students adorning the cover anymore than they want to view flat-chested, anorexic models bearing the latest bikini underwear. Retail deception is all about subliminal distraction. Little more. Otherwise, Publisher's Clearinghouse would not order *six million* "You are one of only *three* finalists" envelopes for their monetary contests.[14]

Like most professionals, an assassin simply needs to endure their chosen profession and retain enough stamina to confront unexpected obstacles. Parachuting into hazardous terrain or emerging from the depths of the sea with an oxygen rebreather are definitely *not* attributes of your professional assassin as

---

[14] Memorandum for the record, 1993, R.J. Godlewski.

they do not represent actions ordinarily undertaken by large segments of the human population and "fitting in" represents the assassin's primary method of disguise. To accomplish this, he or she requires more than the frail physique of a pop star. They may need to tail a target on foot for hours on end without growing tired and fatigued (which may become noticed by an astute observer). They may need to remain idle at a particular location for the same duration waiting patiently for their quarry to arrive. They may also need to blend into the background upon a golf course, within a gymnasium, serve aboard a sailing yacht, or engage within a host of functions that may wind an ordinary individual.

If endurance and disguise are important, then simply pumping irons at the local gym remains impractical (unless required as part of one's disguise). For one thing, professional assassins never remain stationary long enough to frequent a gym. Secondly, public gyms (not to mention the purchase or rental of gym equipment) tend to leave paper and digital trails that may compromise the professional's identity and location (more on this within another chapter). Exercise within a *specific* location permits others to *recognize* an individual through repetition and habit.

An assassin may be a neighbor, but neighbors generally do not offer large volumes of strangers upon their property as would a physical fitness club. This exposure to varied individuals is what comprises the identity of the professional. He or she must always represent a phantom wading through a sea of identities and locations on a constant basis. Therefore, he or she must condition themselves physically *while conducting his or her daily function*. Physical conditioning, for the astute professional, simply becomes part of their *existencia total* much as how they continually consume knowledge.

A professional's mind absorbs information and his body

simply conditions itself through daily activities. Neither of these are relegated to fixed schedules of time as would that for someone trying to lose a few pounds on a New Year's resolution or a student cramming for a final exam. An assassin may be required to sprint to safety over several obstacles should the "unforeseeable" (and there is *always* unforeseeable events) occur and must *never* be caught within a position of ignorance. This is not to say that he or she may have to leap between 70-story high-rises or conduct emergency thoracic surgery, but it does mean that they should be able to communicate with the local taxi driver or answer questions regarding personal preferences when transiting a museum exhibit.

To be caught within a baseball stadium ignorant of what constitutes a double play is just as bad as reaching a fast moving stream and fearing a way of treading the water. The assassin need not be a "know it all", but he or she must know what is *required* of him or her during any moment in their daily life. Therefore, physical condition remains as necessary as mental condition for the mind and body reflect cooperative elements of the human soul. And, ultimately, physical conditioning directly correlates to the ability to deceive and disguise.

Few people scrutinize someone walking alongside the road or through a parking lot. Few even scrutinize someone wearing a suit hurrying into a building or scaling the stairs. These rather innocuous situations permit the assassin to gain exercise while wearing non-PT clothing. In other words, if part of your job requires running in a suit (without building up a deep and *noticeable* sweat), then employ every opportunity to condition yourself while wearing a suit (or dress, or...). Conditioning does not necessarily mean running marathons; it may mean something as simple as moving quickly out of an area where you just bumped off the Grand duke of Fenwick.

Remember, unlike military personnel (or even government agents, for that matter), professional assassins are required to conduct and get away with things the rest of civilized society could not even comprehend and *getting away* with it requires astute measures to conceal oneself no matter the location or situation. This requires the physical fitness to endure a challenging life with as mediocre a body as so not to draw attention to oneself.

One curious example, which works well, say, in the tropics has an assassin wear a scuba weight belt around his waist while within the hotel room. This permits the individual to condition his muscles to endure upwards of 20+ additional pounds on his frame as well as allows for a quick "disconnect" should someone arrive at the door. Most visitors would probably ignore a weight belt lying on the table or a chair. Incidentally, a lead weight makes for a opportunistic weapon with which to crack one's skull. Lead, obviously, can be melted down, virtually destroying any forensic evidence in the process. Or, alternatively, that "innocent" weight belt lying on the chair may not consist of lead weights at all. They could consist of *gold* weights spray painted to appear as if made of lead (more on this within the chapter on money laundering).

Even the furniture within the hotel room may serve as counterweights for quickly increasing muscle tone without drawing attention. Often, the arms of the chair, edge of the bed, or even the handicap rails in the bathroom can be employed to increase the effectiveness of pushups. All the human body requires to build muscle tone is a simple barrier to push off of.

Perhaps the best all-around form of exercise, however, has to involve that swimming pool that even lower end motels possess to varying degrees of cleanliness. Swimming entails the most intense physical exercise known and conditions not only all available muscles, but benefits breathing and blood circulation as well. And, usually ignored by the general population, swimming aids in concealing one's identity admirably (do you *always* recognize people swimming within your local pool?). It had been remarked once, by someone knowledgeable within the field, that ~90% of the human population bears no clue as to the variety of physical exercises available that do not require any special equipment.[15] You can bet that the professional assassin is definitely *not* amongst this large population.

What Good is a Strong Body if You Cannot Hide?

You have just shot a prominent bank executive who had been laundering funds for an international cartel (you would not be a *decent* assassin if you shot one of the "good guys", now would you?) and you need to escape. Between you and your safe house (or safe destination of merit), stands 4.5 million people of a large city, any one of which represents a dire threat to your survival. How do you, the professional assassin, make it to that safe location *and* retrieve your belongings for a trip to the airport (bad idea), port (better idea), or unsecured portion of the border (best idea)?

For starters, your post-assassination safe house will *not* be the one that you had left to embark upon the hit. Assassins *never* follow the same route back to the same location. This represents Security 101. Well, it may be applicable for some personal protection detail that needs to bring their Principal back to the same hotel for a series of conferences, but that Principal probably did not just whack I.M. Narcomoneybags. The assassin's version of Murphy's Law, however, leaves little to error. Therefore, the professional killer probably maintains *several* hotel rooms and other secure locations throughout his area of operations, which also explains why he or she does not

---

[15] Memorandum for the record, R.J. Godlewski.

work for peanuts.

Getting back to your escape, just how do *you* reach that safe location knowing that you just murdered one of the city's (or nation's) most prominent and, possibly, notorious individuals? Easy. You conform to the following rules of conduct.

An Assassin's Fundamental Laws for Escape.

1. *Do not leave a digital footprint.* Throughout the course of the mission, professional assassins do not make purchases or pay for services with credit cards, bank transfers, or any other electronic transfer of funds. They do not use "frequent traveler" cards, cell phones, or retailer discount cards. More importantly, professional assassins know how to avoid the multitude of video surveillance devices through which they must travel.

2. *Do not return to the original location.* Once an assassination takes place, the professional relocates to a new location, one previously stocked with clothing, identity documents, and such other equipment and supplies that facilitate egress from the immediate vicinity. Their mode of transport usually rests with public transportation (more witnesses, less observers) or some form of "disposable" conveyance (remember, automobiles leave beyond a treasure trove of forensic evidence).

3. *Alternate appearances often.* Identities do not have to change, but appearances must. Disposal of an outer garment, a shift of eyeglasses, the aforementioned washing away of an enhanced mustache all represent minor adaptations of appearance that, with the aid of a lackadaisical population, yield significant returns on the investment of effort. Nothing quirky, just practical.

26

Assuming that you did not shoot your victim within the confines of his hotel room surrounded by his protection detail (who are, it is hoped, trained professionals who can notice even the brand of your neck tie by its color), your potential for escape remains sound. Of course, being the *professional*, you were able to partake of several ironies of the human population. The first of these involve crowds. While it is not advisable to operate where many witnesses abound, crowds tend to confuse and distort perceptions.

For every reliable witness, for instance, there remain dozens of those who cannot remember distinct details. Moreover, nobody ever remembers the same fact and most divert to some preconceived notion of what they saw. Therefore, large groups of people will offer large quantities of gratuitous misinformation. If you are even noticed, you may very well be dismissed as "just one of a number of possible leads." Professional assassins employ this collective confusion as an effective force-multiplier.

Another beneficial human condition remains the panic factor. During any form of shooting, particularly one taking place within a crowd, most of those in attendance simply panic. That your target was a notoriously corrupt individual affiliated with a dangerous drug cartel probably makes everyone in attendance a bit paranoid. It also suggests that there are probably no cameras around either, which means that *any* observation of your own presence must be culled from the frail minds of this paranoid – and soon to be panicked – crowd.

A third irony of the human condition rests within both mirror-imaging and pattern recognition. The former simply means that we project our thoughts and expectations upon other individuals. For instance, we find ourselves saying things such as, "If *I* had all that money, I would..." This factor

27

contaminates the intelligence field as well as our spies and counterintelligence agents often sacrifice national security because they view the enemy as kindred souls playing the same game by the same precise rules. The latter characteristic of pattern recognition ranges across a broad perspective of potentialities. For our purposes, however, we will restrict its use to security awareness and criminal application.

Mention a shooting, and most people envision a shooter possessing a handgun or, perhaps, even an "assault rifle" – anything that, to them, *resembles* a firearm that their conscious mind can readily identify. You, being the professional, however, possibly employed an attaché gun, which 99% of the human population would quickly identify as an ordinary piece of executive luggage. Alternatively, you may have employed a pen gun or other simple device that, again, the crowd in attendance would have attributed to any number of innocuous items that everyone in attendance would have possessed under the circumstances.

Your disguised weapon permitted you to 1.) enter the premise without raising concerns; 2.) permitted you to kill the target effectively, and 3.) provided you with a means of escape by following the mad rush to exit the premise (if you had a "normal" firearm, *someone* might have attempted to tackle you). Disguises – human or technical – are not meant to conceal your presence forever. Rather, disguises are meant to buy a particular individual *time* – and, after having pulled off a one-in-a-million killing, your primary consideration is possessing enough time to vacate the premises and launching your 'escape and evasion' plan.

Of course, the foregoing, very simplistic scenario is merely intended to expose to you some aspects of the assassin's trade. A *real* professional would not kill via gun – at least within such a crowded location where scrutiny of an individual's personal possessions increases exponentially with the paranoia of the target. A much easier – and more effective – instrument of destruction would have been a slow-acting poison slipped into the target's drink, food, or applied during an opportunistic handshake. A flattened piece of polyethylene tubing, sealed at the ends with a pinhole orifice at one, can contain a lethal dose of any number of poisons. Held between the index finger and thumb, it can hide unnoticed within even an opened hand and a slight squeeze will squirt the entire contents out.

A handshake here or an obscure wave above a drink or piece of food and the victim can be poisoned without anyone becoming aware of the event. Only federal governments and Hollywood blow up an entire building or crash a crowded airliner just to off a particular individual. Entering a room waving a pistol or, worse, a rifle is going to create too much commotion to go unnoticed. Remember, there are about 6,000+ unsolved murders within the United States each year. Many simply do not get investigated because of personnel and resource shortages. *However*, just about every case of "terrorism" is investigated and if, for example, the government or police botch an investigation of an explosion or an airliner crash does not mean that a journalist or 'conspiracy freak' somewhere will not pick up the hunt.

A professional assassin does not bear marketability if he or she spends all of their time looking over their shoulder. Planning a successful hit takes up enough time as it is. Disguises and deception, therefore, remain integrated into the assassin's entire mission. For example, did the assassin within the foregoing example (you, in this case), simply pull out a zip gun and shoot the banker between the eyes as he was toasting his good fortune to be so corrupted? Or did the assassin manage to spike his martini with a powerful toxin while he was clinking toasts with his other unmentionable associates?

In reality, a more likely scenario (one that you probably did not consider) would employ several aspects of disguise and deception for which we just discussed. Entering the location under the guise of a friendly media organization, the assassin had before prepared several modified pencils to serve as smoke grenades. The middle of each "moderately used" pencil was carefully drilled out in order to insert a small amount of zinc dust and hexachloroethane into the cavity.[16]Underneath the metallic cap, within a hollowed out portion beneath the erasers, rests the 'match' igniter.

These pencil smoke grenades do not produce a large quantity of smoke nor do they burn for any length of time. What they do, however, is provide just enough white smoke for "someone" to notice and where there is smoke rising within *different* locations, there "may" be fire. Even if panic does not set in, the Principal's security detail will likely escort him away from the commotion into a safe area. Here, is where the astute assassin with the powerful toxin within his now-gloved hand (within the polyethylene tube between his thumb and figure) innocently bumps against the banker as his security team moves him out of the area.

Before long, the banker will become sick and die. No one, within the clearing of the room, noticed the assassin do anything other than move out of the threat location with the rest of the crowd. No fingerprints will compromise his identify, no photographs appear of his innocuous touching of the victim, and no serial numbers verify his purchases. He simply moves out of the location and, feigning agitated nerves, simply retreats outside for "some fresh air" and disappears through a preplanned pattern of altering disguises (not to be confused with *identities*) and moves on with his life.

---

[16] Tenney L. Davis, *The Chemistry of Powder and Explosives* (Las Vegas: Angriff Press, 2010), 123.

The Five-Minute Disguise.

Because death and killing represent broad and complex subjects, which we shall discuss later within appropriate chapters, they consume a great deal of time on the part of the assassin. This cuts into his or her ability to develop and employ disguises. Like everything else in life, experience builds a repertoire on which future manifestations are built (which is why college, for instance, comes after 13 years of preparatory schooling). Nevertheless, the professional killer offers a pattern of behavior that permits this experience to flourish. Nowhere is this more important than within the field of disguises.

Consider this. An experienced corporate executive and a novice interviewee are both dressed similarly, but appear very much different in composure.[17]Despite that they could be wearing the exact same clothing, the executive's attire seems to conform to his body whereas the person seeking the job definitely looks out of place.[18]This is because the experienced executive probably wears a suit everyday and has for years whereas the applicant only pulls his suit out of the closet whenever he has an interview. Both *situation* and location bear upon how an individual is perceived by observers.

People have been comprised by a pair of shoelaces. This may not appear to be a valid security threat amongst, say, the United States where clothing is more of a fashion statement than a disguise, but like with the young interviewee, the slightest discrepancy can lead to identification. This becomes even more severe when the individual is passing through a foreign culture where even a wristwatch is noticed. Spies, terrorists, and transnational criminals often fail within their assignments simply because they forgot to replace their very

---

[17] R.J. Godlewski, "Human Intelligence: Perceiving an Enemy's Thoughts." *American Intelligence Journal* 27, no. 1 (2009): 36.

[18] Ibid.

underwear.

To avoid this, the professional assassin bears clothing caches within strategic regions of operation. These articles of clothing are routinely supplemented by additions purchased from time to time (assassins, being people, like to shop too). However, "newness" must be the exception rather than the rule. Again, just like the executive/interviewee scenario, *new* clothing bears all the indicators of being out of place or inexperienced. For this reason, the assassin is likely to visit thrift stores that appear within virtually every large city or inhabited town.

With minimal cash outlays (no credit card purchases!), any individual can acquire a range of "lived in" clothing that matches the cultural expectations of an observing public. Furthermore, the astute assassin (or other criminal of merit) can purchase a range of electronics and home appliances – not to mention, knives, tools, and other "deadly instruments" – bearing a multitude of *local* fingerprints. Plausible deniability works great for more than just governments!

4

TARGET FAMILIARIZATION & WEAPONS SMUGGLING.

Every time an "assassin" is mentioned on the evening news, their weapons inventory betrays their amateurish status.[19] This remains the same problem with so-called "snipers", which the international media seems quick to term anyone shooting a firearm at others from an unknown position. Inasmuch as a true sniper retains far more information than just how to point a rifle at somebody from afar, an assassin is not someone who happens to be caught red-handed with spy 'weapons' or espionage gear. On the contrary, if the international media is laying the charge, then the perpetrator is most likely anyone *but* whom they characterize him or her as.

---

[19] For just the most recent example, visit http://news.yahoo.com/poison-pens-lipstick-guns-8-real-life-spy-153400840.html. Accessed November 2012.

A professional assassin simply does not get caught by the authorities anymore than a professional sniper's actions get noticed by the media. Bearing a "lipstick gun", say, illustrates a fundamental lack of operational awareness[20]; assassins generally do not travel very far with their weapons despite this popularity with Hollywood. The most important reason for this, obviously, remains that the professional does not select an assassination method *until* they decide upon an assassination location. And despite "location, location, location" representing everything in real estate investing, assassins prefer to let the target's own mannerisms, idiosyncrasies, habits, and other foibles provide the best method and location to terminate the subject.

Think of an assassination plan as a two-part, three-dimensional logistics operation, each facet involving a myriad of travel plans, security considerations, weather analyses, personnel encounters, falsehoods and deceptions, and a host of other arrangements a typical individual would not encounter within a lifetime of college courses, career functions, and family responsibilities. When these two facets – one offered by the target and the other experienced by the assassin – intersect is *when* the killing occurs. It is during this precise period when the method, location, and time are actualized and a successful assassination *can* occur. The easiest way to understand this ability is to imagine two baseball players standing at opposite ends of the field (say, at home plate and deep center) and throwing baseballs into the air and hoping that both balls collide.

The Human End of the Target.

Even the most despicable person on the planet remains a human being. In Western, Christianized society this represents

---

[20] Ibid.

a fundamental tenet of existence. Of course, *every* human individual bears an internal death "wish list" however small within the deepest recesses of their mind and this is only natural. They do not actually want to impose upon these people any harm anymore than they actually mean it when they say "touch my daughter again, kid, and I will kill you!" This is not the point.

People will instinctively look upon a story involving a child molester, a street ganger, or even a corrupt politician or capitalist and say "Why is *that* person wasting our precious oxygen supply?" Despite this primal desire, people simply do not go out of their way and kill that particular individual. Most people would, perhaps correctly, assume that once started, the list would grow long and cease only when the individual found him or herself standing alone on terra firma.

Assassins, however, *kill* and kill repeatedly (if not necessarily often). Their devotion to their job remains little different than someone employed to kill animals for meat or a police officer taking the life of someone intent on killing another. The fundamental difference, of course, is that the professional killer has accepted the extrajudicial task of serving as judge, jury, and executioner of another *human individual*, which makes their trade uniquely rare and ghastly effective. This does *not* mean, however, that the assassin kills a complete stranger. On the contrary.

Assassins do not simply pick up a telephone, agree to a contract, and walk out the front door to return within an hour with having taken another individual's life. That's the function of mules who act as 'hit men' for gangs, terrorists, and mafia organizations (each usually employing some form of "house cleaning" with each murder). The professional assassin, to the contrary, becomes very intimate with his or her target before the actual killing takes place. This intimacy revolves around their coming to know their target better than that individual's wife, family, or coworkers. To understand the traveling habits, hobbies, associations, fears, desires, and daily (and weekly, monthly...) schedule of *any* individual is to truly *know* that individual.

This is what separates common murderers from the warmer-blooded and calculating professional killer: a true appreciation of the individual about to die. Only professional military snipers probably come even close to matching this ability and *then* the snipers bear the privilege of having "higher echelons" remove much of the decision-making from their minds. Not so the assassin. He or she accepts an assignment based upon his or her relationship (or lack thereof) with the client and then proceeds to orchestrate the killing of the target. What is *not* revealed within Hollywood movies, unfortunately, is that much of the above surveillance and tracking of the target takes place *before* the assassin ultimately agrees to conduct the mission.

Remember, we are not talking about gang bangers or Mafiosi here. An assassin is about to kill a completely new individual and then, perhaps, go into hiding for several months if not longer depending upon *who*, precisely, they sent packing for the Pearly Gates. Amateurs rush into things. Professionals are not afraid to remark "You want me to kill *who* exactly?" before slamming the door closed behind them.

In fact, as a matter of pure survival, a professional assassin probably has six or seven other "rackets" – businesses, investments, hobbies, school studies, etc. – ongoing to keep their mind and lifestyle intact. A botched assassination attempt will likely disrupt the whole cart. It would be as if a football wide receiver lost his salary, his college education, all endorsements, retirement plan, and wife, kids, and the Cadillac out front of his million-dollar mansion if he but dropped a single catch in the end zone during a preseason game. For this reason, an assassin may represent a risk taker, but he or she is most emphatically *not a gambler*. And the best way of avoiding "drops", is to completely understand the target individual.

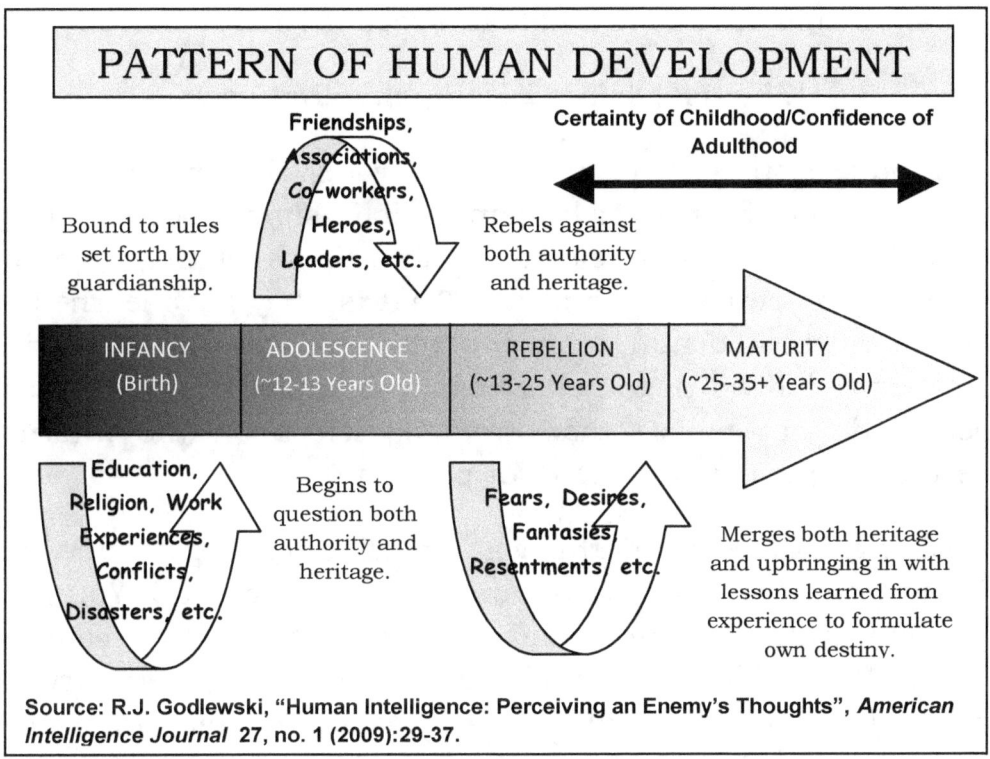

PATTERN OF HUMAN DEVELOPMENT

Friendships, Associations, Co-workers, Heroes, Leaders, etc.

Certainty of Childhood/Confidence of Adulthood

Bound to rules set forth by guardianship.

Rebels against both authority and heritage.

| INFANCY (Birth) | ADOLESCENCE (~12-13 Years Old) | REBELLION (~13-25 Years Old) | MATURITY (~25-35+ Years Old) |

Education, Religion, Work Experiences, Conflicts, Disasters, etc.

Begins to question both authority and heritage.

Fears, Desires, Fantasies, Resentments, etc.

Merges both heritage and upbringing in with lessons learned from experience to formulate own destiny.

Source: R.J. Godlewski, "Human Intelligence: Perceiving an Enemy's Thoughts", *American Intelligence Journal* 27, no. 1 (2009):29-37.

Humans remain quirky, but they can be perceived inasmuch as intimate spouses may, from time to time, finish one another's sentences or retrieve a fresh roll of toilet paper from the hall closet with the minimalist of prompting from the indisposed partner. The above diagram illustrates the profound influences and mental states – both linear and cyclic – that every human individual progresses through from the "certainty of childhood" on through the "confidence of adulthood".

Every individual matures through the same processes, so to possibly understand *any* particular individual, we must first understand the sea of influences that he or she wades through on their way towards maturity (usually not achieved until at least 35 years of age). For the professional assassin, this means developing a significant human intelligence (HUMINT) sourced dossier on the targeted victim. This is a time-consuming function, but by no means difficult in today's age of instant communications and high-speed Internet connections.

The Assassin's Intelligence Network

If professional assassins move through the world largely unnoticed by the rest of humanity, it is simply because they have learned to avoid electronic association with the other seven billion souls on the planet. That is, they have learned to minimize their digital footprint that exposes an otherwise inattentive individual to *permanent* observation by others. Most people do not realize that *anything* left upon the Internet becomes a permanent record for posterity.

Consider the problem this way. Imagine sending a letter to a friend from New York to Los Angeles via postal mail. You seal the letter, affix a stamp, and then drop it into the mailbox. Unless there is someone crooked working for the postal service, your letter arrives at its destination a week later, unopened, and your friend becomes the first person to read your words since you mailed the original document. Now consider the same scenario paralleled with the actions of the Internet.

Once your letter is removed from the mailbox and accepted by the postal service, it is removed from the envelope and a copy is produced before resealing and then forwarded to, say, Chicago. At Chicago, the local postmaster decides that he cannot trust New York, so he removes the letter and makes an additional copy before sending the original letter on to St. Louis. The St. Louis postmaster trusts neither the New York or Chicago workers so he makes a further copy before mailing the letter onto Las Vegas and, eventually, Los Angeles where both actions are repeated. And because nobody can trust anybody within this paranoid system, everyone makes copies of *their* copies. Between you and your friend, a thousand or more people have read your intimate letter before all is said and done and they will continue reading your letter for many decades to come yet.[21]

The Internet facilitates life, yes, but it also compromises personal security exponentially. Every photograph that a worker posts about a company party on a social networking site, for instance, provides an intruder with yet another tidbit of knowledge about the business and its facilities. Alternate reality sites such as *Second Life* provide criminals, terrorists, and other disreputable characters with an opportunity to case the interior of a building or facility without ever having had to visit the location in person.[22]

Technology simply compounds the problem with communications. The U.S. Federal Bureau of Investigation (FBI), for instance, maintains the ability to turn on your cell phone and record your conversations without you ever being aware of these actions.[23] Of course, the FBI requires judicial authorization to conduct such clandestine eavesdropping on, say, your bedroom activities, but what of others who do not hold such value of the law? If the U.S. government bears the capability to undertake a particular action, do not believe for a moment that *nobody else* maintains similar capabilities.

The professional assassin employs such abilities and knows how to work individuals to gain even more information about

---

[21] Memorandum for the record, R.J. Godlewski. A brief abstract for an archaeological conference poster presentation proposed for ~1992 still shows up within Internet searches during 2012, some 20 years after the presentation was supposed to have taken place.

[22] Steven Nutt and Josh Lyons, *Virtual Worlds and Terrorist Attack Planning* (Shawnee, OK: Urban Warfare Analysis Center, August 2008), 4-8.

[23] Memorandum for the record, R.J. Godlewski.

his or her target. Executive protection specialists often conduct advances for foreign locations (not necessarily meaning "international" locations) to scout hotel rooms, plan vehicular routes, and even arrange preparations with domestic security personnel.   They talk (and pay gratuities) to hotel cleaning staff, taxi drivers, bartenders, and delivery personnel to extract as much critical information as possible from the locals to ensure the safe passage and stay of their principal. Assassins have access to this broad range of sources too, and, more often than not, tip heavier than those protecting the executive.

Terrorists and Marxist guerrillas often employ the services of what the rest of the world refers to as "street rabble" – notoriously known as *mousseblin* – to spy upon intruders and other questionable characters.[24] Beggars sit on street corners and observe the whole of the boulevard, newspaper venders spy on the entrance of the hotel across the street, and delivery boys on bicycles keep abreast of traffic conditions. Pedestrians from all categories of cleanliness, austerity, and virtue can be bought – if the price is right.

If the assassin's target is a powerful business executive, then *someone* bears a grudge against this individual and such grievances open them to prospects of harming that individual. They do not even have to be paid; most disgruntled people are quite willing to announce their grievances and complaints openly on the Web. Social networking sites – including all those that you have heard about (we do not need to name names here) – bear fundamental security violations within their software programs. An individual with appropriate computer knowledge can employ your [name your favorite social site here] account to activate your computer's video camera without you even knowing about it.

---

[24] Paul Balor, *Manual of the Mercenary Soldier* (Boulder: Paladin Press, 1988) 238-244.

The reason that it takes the professional assassin so long to plot their attack rests largely with the sheer availability of information regarding their intended victim. Naturally, of course, most targets are not mild-mannered citizens careless about their personal security. Nevertheless, even national leaders compromise themselves through casual errors in protocol, scheduling, or spontaneity. The assassin, like the vulture or terrorist, waits patiently for just such screw-up's.

Many people should be committed to an insane asylum for the paper trail that these individuals leave. They sign up for "Frequent Flyer" programs, discount cards at their local grocery store, email notices from virtually every Internet site they visit, and – horror of all horrors – use a credit or check card to pay for every purchase they make. If they knew how much *money* was made through the selling and sharing of personal information, most people would go into catatonic fits. Sadly, such profits mean that *your* personal information is being shared whether you want it shared or not.

Before a professional assassin even moves into the ambush location, he or she already knows the medical condition of the victim, what clothing he is likely wearing, who he calls most frequently on the cell phone, what vehicle they will be riding in, what hotel room they will be sleeping in, and when their flight – be it commercial or corporate – is due to land. Yes, the target's protective services detail will go through extraordinary measures to conceal this information, but they have to defend against *infinite* threats. The assassin needs only concentrate on *one particular individual.*

More importantly, a protected individual's security team may have dozens of trips to arrange and prepare for through several cities within the United States (if the principal is American) and beyond. The professional assassin, however, can isolate selected locations for merit, choose an appropriate time (say, during an overnight layover) when the security detail may be compromised by an infinite variety of activities, and plan for the "one time" when all the cards line up for an effective and secure strike. Proper utilization of available intelligence permits this planning. What involves considerably more effort, however, remains locating an appropriate tool of assassination and getting it to where the attack will take place.

A World Awash with Weapons and Yet So Few to be Found.

Mafia and gang-related killers are often depicted shooting some poor slob between the eyes and then casually tossing the firearm into a river and walking away as if not possessing a care in the world. The problem with this particular scenario is that tossed guns can *still* be found and that bullets (and, perhaps, shell casings) still bear forensic evidence. That movies and television shows illustrate this activity has more to do with convenience and entertainment than anything else and, for the most part, they simply seek to illuminate the activities of a "killer" and not necessarily someone who actually kills for a living.

This book about professional assassins, however, is not meant to entertain or elevate the romanticism of killers. Its intention is to illuminate the many facets of their trade and, hopefully, shed some of the misconceptions about professional killing (insofar as practical, ethical, and desirable). For this reason, if little else, simply discussing a killer affixing a suppressor (a.k.a., "silencer") to a .45 caliber pistol and shooting someone in the back does not take much thought as virtually every pulp fiction author, CSI-show writer, and trashy tabloid journalist comes to the same tactic within their own work.

A *professional* assassin, to the contrary, knows that a package of a specific-variety chocolate pudding mix, a syringe filled with a common household chemical, and a microwave oven makes for one fairly powerful, pressure sensitive explosive that when laid upon a table with a heavy book on top of the package will cause a propelling shockwave that *could* snap a person's neck once the book (i.e., projectile) is lifted. Sure, one has to accommodate some plausible story for *why* a package of chocolate pudding mix is lying underneath a book on a table, but before they consider the options, the victim is probably dead and the police are left looking for an "explosive" that caused the blast. So much more interesting, say, than shooting someone in the back with a traceable bullet.

This simply illustrates the conundrum of the professional assassin: weapons are *everywhere*, they just need to be transported safely and secretively to the point of assassination. Herein is where the *professional* distinguishes themselves from the rank amateurs that populate Hollywood, television, and the streets of the city nearest to you. Weapons selection, accordingly, remains just as important as weapons smuggling and both determine the assassination inasmuch as the assassination determines the weapon of choice.

Recognizable firearms are very difficult to conceal, particularly when one has to travel via airline and other public conveyances. Similarly, explosives bear indicators that can point back to origins of purchase and leave behind too much destruction affecting innocent parties. The Israelis killed Hussain Abu-Khair in 1973 by placing an explosive charge underneath his Nicosia, Cyprus hotel bed.[25] The resulting explosion blew both his body and the hotel room apart, leaving literary material for decades afterwards. A professional assassin is doomed if he or she follows suit.

To escape publicity of their crime, assassins need to conceal

---

[25] Aaron J. Klein, *Strike Back: The 1972 Munich Olympics Massacre and Israel's Deadly Response* (New York: Random House, 2007), 138.

both their presence and that of whatever tool they employ to kill their victim. One can kill with a ball peen hammer, yes, but hammers are hard to discard and bear microscopic forensic evidence if located. A better choice would be a garrote fashioned from 100-pound test monofilament fishing line that can be melted into a miniscule ball after the killing and discarded many miles away. Poisons work as effectively, but containers can retain compromising evidence too, which is why the aforementioned polyethylene tube serves well. As with the fishing line garrote, it can be melted after the liquid is discharged.

Firearms bear a bit more discretion and, therefore, the best options involve those devices that do not appear or function as traditional firearms. A .22 caliber gun incorporated into the handle of a briefcase offers concealment in both design and operation. An assassin operating such a device only needs to act as if a "terrified bystander" for the ruse to work; nobody would notice an assassin amongst a group of fleeing executives. A similar device involves a pen gun or perhaps a loaded cigarette lighter, but here the actions of the assassin might attract attention from the more observant or any cameras in presence.

Long-rifles offer the advantage of distance, but are normally frowned upon by skilled assassins for they offer little secrecy and, again, bullets leave forensic evidence behind. Two options work within the assassin's favor. The first rests with a high-speed frangible bullet that can pass through the victim's body and then disintegrate upon impacting anything hard.[26]The second option involves using a sabot round within a larger caliber cartridge; this itself offers two distinct choices of either employing a 'clean' bullet with no rifling marks, or a previously

---

[26] John West, *Fry the Brain: The Art of Urban Sniping and its Role in Modern Guerrilla Warfare* (Countryside, VA: SSI, 2008), 383.

used bullet with compromising markings from another shooter.[27]

There remains, of course, the problem of a rifle appearing as if a rifle, but the astute assassin does not possess a "favorite" weapon and, unlike hunters and collectors, does not become attached to any particular firearm. For this reason, he or she is likely to custom-build a firearm specifically for the job at hand (shootings ostensibly representing a *tailored* assassination, usually of a prominent military or political leader). The better option remains a shotgun which, despite its much shorter range, can affect an assassination without the need for barrel rifling or leaving behind much forensic evidence. A simple device could be constructed within virtually any tubular frame, such as that of a wheelchair, umbrella, crutch, or cane.

Moving firearms, explosives, poisons, and other deadly devices takes advantage of both human proclivity for identifying things that appear "natural" to the eye and the myriad of commercial and industrial objects that contain crevices, voids, and other cavities within which any number of devices can be secreted. It was not by coincidence that many "old school" arms smugglers began life with agricultural degrees. Entire assemblages of "monster guns" have been covertly shipped from one end of the planet to the other under varying descriptions of industrial or agricultural goods. Ballistic missiles too.

Barrels and bottles full of liquids, ranging from 55-gallon oil drums to innocuous jugs of milk, can be employed to smuggle even the most vicious of substances. Who notices a gallon of milk (particularly if that milk contains a weighted packet of white poison secreted inside)? If gold can be spray painted and covered with engine grease to be hidden within a range of

---

[27] Ibid.

other, legitimate engine parts (see next chapter), why not rifle barrels, explosive components, and even knives, hatchets, and swords? During the Second World War, explosives were fashioned into lumps of coal, secured within the carcass of dead animals, and even turned into a form of edible pancake mix. Why? Because a single lump of coal cast amongst thousands of others, for example, disrupts the human demands of attention and conscientious observation.

A shopper notices an elderly passerby seated within a wheelchair and oxygen being applied to their nose from a green tank located at the back of the chair. Does *anyone* suspect anything other than oxygen? Suppose the tank contained firearms, explosives, or even a small-yield nuclear weapon? What percentage of shoppers bother to inspect the oxygen canister at sufficiently close range to notice that the top (or, far more likely, the bottom) screws on? And what of the multitude of tubing that comprises the wheelchair itself? Could not such framing contain an infinite amount of concealable weaponry?

We have discussed a range of killing devices from the inefficient (compromised chocolate pudding powder) to the effective (a fishing line garrote). Each offers an unique set of possibilities, but no method of death bears as much potential as the simple "accident", such as when a target *mysteriously* falls down a flight of stairs or drowns within a swimming pool. Death, and its various causes, has yet to be discussed. For now, we still need to understand the many aspects of the assassin's *business.*

5

INTERNATIONAL BUSINESS AND MONEY LAUNDERING.

O nly governments can print money...legally. Everyone else must earn it...legally or not. Wealth in the form of capital currency obeys the laws of supply and demand. He who possesses a product or service that another requires can generally set his price. Only when competition arises do prices for these products and services fall to levels that are more acceptable to the consumer. Monopolies, formed by either cartels or governments, seek to restrict competition for the sake of maximum profit. That is, the antithesis of free market enterprise remains either crime or regulation, both of which serve the same purpose – corruption of the natural flow of humanity.[28]

The professional assassin is a capitalist, despite his or her

---

[28] R.J. Godlewski, "Financing of Terrorism", *Tactical Extractions Counterterrorism Paper* 07 (2010): 1.

trade representing an illegal one. He or she offers a required service that very few others are willing to provide, assumes all risks and challenges in providing just such a service (on a no-cure, no-pay arrangement[29]), and seeks a maximum profit based upon their "unique" qualifications and capabilities. Governments and criminal organizations try their best to regulate and restrict the service of death, but they cannot cease independent entrepreneurs from participating within what remains very much a free market

For this reason, the *independent contractor* assassin must wear all the various business hats of their enterprise, from floor sweeper on up through chief executive officer. It remains a business ripe with international financial transactions, foreign competition, a multitude of indigenous languages and cultures, arranging retirement "plans", and, oh yes, groups of people who want to employ capital punishment if they lay hands upon you.

Without care, assassination promises to be a very brief and unprofitable business. Furthermore, like many other individualistic criminal enterprises, the professional killer must isolate himself from both international and domestic law enforcement investigation. This often requires building a global corporate shell around his or her operations, presenting the assassin with the semblance of an honorable – if somewhat reclusive – business executive while shielding their livelihood from even the most intense scrutiny. That is, at worst, the successful assassin represents the one who everyone in the world believes "could" be a professional killer and, yet, *no one* can actually prove it.

---

[29] No-cure, no-pay arrangements are utilized in industries such as maritime salvage where the salvage company receives no pay unless they "cure" the wreck, stranding, or disabled vessel.

Nevertheless, the *best* assassins in the world represent those who do not even cross the radar of any nation's federal or domestic law enforcement agencies. They do not associate with criminal elements, avoid breaking laws within the country of their citizenship, and never, *ever* travel without bona fide commercial reasons (frequent "tourism" raises far too many questions, particularly if the assassin finds a need to be in situ for any length of time).

The Company Man (or Woman).

It remains far easier to employ one cover organization than several haphazard ones. For this reason, the particularly successful assassin does not chance employing numerous deceptive covers, flirting around dangerously with various identities as within many Hollywood movies and television shows. The advent of facial recognition software and joint-intelligence fusion centers eliminates such fanciful deception. Therefore, practicality and common sense rule the day. Again, the subtle shifts in apparel that disrupt casual observers remains the best practice.

What *is* required, however, is an organizational structure that permits the assassin to transit several locations and duties without arousing suspicion. This usually involves a singular offshore corporation that "owns" numerous onshore corporations throughout the world. For instance, the assassin may elect to establish a Nevis corporation for asset protection and personal security. This corporation, in turn, may own corporations in Europe, America, and Asia. Banking would be handled through a numbered account in Zurich, Central America, or the Cayman Islands and even if those accounts are compromised, they are managed by the Nevis corporation shielding the true owner from further scrutiny.

In America, for example, the parent corporation may own a subsidiary in South Dakota, a relatively normal state that offers, amongst other benefits, no personal state income tax, few restrictive gun laws (for practicing, testing, etc.), and no state requirements for licensing of security companies (which could aid in several aspects of the assassin's trade). Wherever the assassin chooses to establish his or her core enterprise, nothing works effectively unless it is secured by dozens of overlapping systems designed to confuse prying eyes.

Like a telephone call bounced around the planet to disrupt tracing, multiple bank accounts and corporations serve to challenge anyone seeking to get a handle on the assassin's business. At a minimum, simultaneous entities and accounts make it virtually impossible to trace the location of the assassin, particular when numerous safe houses and residences are employed (see Chapter 6). Speaking of telephones, professional assassins do no employ cell telephones, even those of the disposable, pre-paid variety – cellular communications can be taped, scouted, and compromised.

The best cover businesses are usually considered those within the import/export or tourism industries where an individual can travel extensively without arousing suspicion. The problem with these businesses, however, is that they often require significant facilities and/or staffs that offer opportunities for compromise and/or subversion. Fortunately, for the assassin, there remain numerous businesses that permit discretion without generating suspicion:

- *Artistic enterprises*. Posing as an artist or photographer permits a professional killer to travel without the need to be accompanied by large staffs. Photography offers the opportunity to perform reconnaissance missions around the target whereas working as a painter, for instance, permits the individual to remain at one location for many hours or days as the "artist" paints the scene, sunset, or whatever has attracted his or her eye;

- **Non-Profit Organization**. Most people incorrectly assume that a not-for-profit enterprise represents a charitable, tax-exempt organization that provides some form of community benefit. To the contrary, a non-profit corporation simply represents a business that offers *no profits* to its ownership (which could represent members, shareholders, or simply serve as a self-owned entity). By forgoing the tax-exempt status, the assassin simply works as an employee for a corporation that bears no ownership, no contributors, and need not maintain any formal address (save for, like all corporations, a registered agent office that can be contracted out to any number of 'incorporate yourself' services online). In fact, *most* of the assassin's corporate facilities represent "virtual offices" that look, sound, and 'feel' as if legitimate offices but are actually owned and operated by business services corporations.[30]

- **Courier**. A courier is an individual that transports a package or letter in person. Such a person, for instance, may hand deliver important business documents, precious gems or jewelry, or any other item that a client does not want to leave to the care of an international package delivery company or a governmental postal service. While there may be problems involved with actually serving a client, a well-covered assassin may simply represent a courier for one of his many offshore entities.

---

[30] Any entrepreneur can rent a business address, a telephone number with a receptionist, a conference room for a few hours per month, and mail reception/forwarding for a nominal fee per month in cities located in virtually every nation.

- **_Yachting_**. Hundreds of individuals from virtually ever seagoing nation (and even those landlocked countries) sail around the world aboard sailing vessels and motor yachts. As these individuals range from those who need to 'work' their passage from one port to another on through multi-billionaires in retirement, no one ever suspects a reason for their existence. Although precise itineraries are difficult to schedule, such travel remains extremely valuable for the professional killer as yachts are self-contained residences, sanctuaries, and training facilities (the ocean is a mighty large place to let loose a few rounds without anyone noticing) all rolled up into one nice, neat, concealable package.

Whatever business (or businesses) the assassin chooses, the cover likely remains his or her core occupation between missions. Therefore, the appropriate cover generally follows a field which the assassin understands rather intimately.

The fundamental key, nevertheless, remains that any cover operation appear both plausible _and_ acceptable. If mere shoelaces, as was discussed previously, can compromise an individual operating within a foreign culture, then nothing remains inconsequential in developing a major cover operation. Accordingly, if an assassin is employing the photographer disguise, then he or she must actually _function_ as a photographer. There must be avenues for which he or she may sell their photographs, perhaps even an exhibit. If they function as a writer, then there must be books (probably _not_ like this one) available for purchase or other writings proudly displayed within magazines, academic journals, or newspapers.

This is, of course, common sense and the reader would be quite reasonable in raising this observation. However, that "professional assassins" are even discussed within the newspaper proves beyond a doubt that violations of this fundamental rule occur in more than just Hollywood action flicks. If, for whatever extraordinary reason an assassin should find himself compromised, he could immediately deflect such accusations with a spontaneous, "Hey, if I were an assassin, do you think *for one damn moment* that I would be peddling my way on a shoestring budget snapping photographs of silly old men feeding ducks at the park?" Or, perhaps, she would just as quickly say "Oh, *that's* a good one! Can you please tell my editor that so that he will put me on the crime beat instead of wasting my time covering New Age restaurants?"

An executive cover would be even easier to employ. "Who *has time* to be an assassin? Do you think that my wife would have left me for the mailman had I actually possessed such an exciting job?" You get the picture; an assassin's job is 90% cover, 10% killing. Rather, 99% lying, 1% being the most lethal individual on the planet. There simply do not remain enough (authentic) contracts available to devote everyday of the year to the trade, so each "mission" becomes a lifestyle unto its own. In fact, assassins pretty much spend most of their time trying to keep their money secure and available for the future.

Of Dead Presidents and Hectic Cleansing.

As with all living organisms, commercial institutions require a "life blood" to fuel growth through a return on investment, dispense energy through capital enterprise, and protect against infection through confidentiality and liquidity.[31] Nowhere is this more important than those businesses that aid and support the professional assassin. More so, perhaps, than any other criminal enterprise, the individual professional killer must operate his or her extrajudicial affairs alone and in direct confrontation with the world – be that community civilized or

---

[31] R.J. Godlewski, "Financial Counterintelligence: Fractioning the Lifeblood of Asymmetrical Warfare" *American Intelligence Journal* 29, no. 2 (2011): 24.

criminal. That is, in a world full of sharks and guppies, the assassin rests as little more than fresh bait.

To defend against this sea of carnivorous threats and operate peacefully (as peacefully as any professional killer can aspire to), the assassin must secure their operation from the broader world and this, more than anything else, requires effective methods of cleansing illicit funds into those "honorably" obtained. As good a killer as he or she may be, they must be *better* at laundering money, particularly in this post-9/11 world of terrorism paranoia.

Moving large amounts of illicit funds (assassins do not work for minimum wage) between nations raises a host of challenges from international banking laws to domestic tax obligations to safety and storage issues. Several options, however, remain available for the astute assassin. The best option remains gold, which can be melted down and molded into an infinite number of shapes and sizes and disguised as virtually any three-dimensional object such as engine crankshafts (covered with grease, of course), nuts and bolts (spray painted), and ceramic statues (covered with a fine layer of clay). The beauty of gold remains that only a professional metallurgist bears the experience to determine the purity of any metallic element.

Gems and jewelry represent the second best choice for laundering funds because, as with gold, it requires an experienced eye and discerning professional to adequately determine the *true* value of any particular gemstone or article of jewelry. A jewel encrusted broach, for instance, may appear to be worth, say, $2,500, but fetch only $300 from any discriminating buyer. The $2,200 discrepancy would not flag any attention from an inexperienced customs officer, leading to further opportunities within trade-based, value-added money laundering.

Nearly $500 *billion* in "dirty money" moves through the United States annually via irregularly priced trade goods. These include $153 dishtowels imported from Pakistan and $1,500 bulldozers exported from the United States to Colombia.[32]Illicit currency exchanges, such as the Colombian Black Market Peso Exchange (BMPE) provide a quick and efficient method for laundering monies throughout the world as local residents are often distrustful of their own government.[33]Utilizing unofficial money transfers such as the *Hawala* system widespread throughout the Middle East and Asia eliminates a digital trail altogether.

---

[32] John A. Cassara, *Hide & Seek: Intelligence, Law Enforcement, and the Stalled War on Terrorist Finance* (Washington: Potomac Books, 2006), 231.

[33] Ibid, 141-143.

Another method that the astute assassin can employ in trading ill-gotten monies for legitimate cash remains owning cash-based businesses such as hair salons, topless bars, and those perennial gold mines known as payday 'cash advance' retailers (unofficially known as "licensed" loan sharks). People working near the low end of social economic classes often have to borrow funds to survive until their next paycheck at astronomically high interest rates. At the other end of the morality scale include check-cashing services that will gladly cash your check as long as you walk out the door with a few hundred dirty dollars needing to be recycled back into society.

The opportunity to launder money rests as infinite as the human spirit that seeks to transfer large sums of 'investment' capital without tipping off the authorities. From stolen automobiles, that can be shipped to the Middle East where corrupt customs officials can "authenticate" local ownership to textiles where "re-branded" clothing can reap millions in profits, these avenues of deception range far greater than even American attempts to corral them. Combined with numbered bank accounts, bearer-certificate owned offshore corporations, and virtually no nation with a secured border, and the opportunities for the assassin to cycle his or her finances freely around the planet remain both numerous and secretive.

6

SAFE HAVENS, SECURE COMMUNICATIONS, AND ESCAPE AND EVASION PLANS.

Eventually, numbered offshore accounts can be discovered, bearer-certificate holders can be indentified, and national borders guarded by the presence of a lucky agent or two. It might take several years, but Murphy's Law applies to the assassination profession as well as every other human endeavor. The slightest miscalculation here or the gravest challenge there tears into an otherwise well-orchestrated plan and *improvisation* returns in an effort to snatch victory out of the jaws of defeat. Here is where the professionals separate themselves from the amateurs, criminal thugs, and other wannabes.

Hollywood often glosses over the tripartite requirements of safe havens, secure communications, and Escape & Evasion (E&E) because, frankly, an hour or two on the screen remains insufficient time in which to include otherwise monotonous and repetitive topics. Remember, the reason that Hollywood

57

movies and television shows are routinely picked on here rests because they border upon impracticality at best and fantasy at worst. Motion pictures and television serials are designed to entertain – *not* educate – for commercial advertisers are paying for you to be glued to the tube (remember that aforementioned Viagra® advertisement. A bunch of guys parroting Elvis Presley remains more "entertaining" than simply discussing the problems associated with erectile dysfunction).

Three of Hollywood's most egregious errors regarding professional assassins include:

- *Former U.S. Special Operations Forces (SOF) training.* First, U.S. special forces (including Army Green Berets, Navy SEALS, Delta Force, CIA paramilitary, etc.) do *not* train in assassinations. Not after the Pike and Church committee hearings of the 1970s. Most are now involved within sanctioned "targeted killings" and drone attacks that more approximate military actions than one-on-one hunter-killer missions that break the bounds of bureaucratic oversight. Second, people with the kind of military/federal training that *could* become assassins are observed with the greatest of care by domestic and international agencies. Not exactly the kind of background that highly secretive clients (do *not* believe for a moment that the U.S. government retains secrets) seek;

- *Use of personal homes as operational centers.* We have all seen the "good guys" raid an assassin's home and, through CSI-trickery or simply "discovery" of a wall safe or some form of unique hiding place (hollowed out mattresses appear to be a favorite), the assassin's *true* lifestyle is figured out. Complete and utter rubbish. No professional killer worth his or her fee is ever going to compromise their home by keeping files, records, weapons, or any other compromising information regarding his or her career present. Both technology and law enforcement experience is making cache hiding a very difficult chore. If someone is even considered to be a professional killer, the police will not think twice about razing the house to the ground in order to find every hiding place imaginable. If houses could be made secure, then governments would find no problem in letting employees take home compromising information;

- *Murders that lead directly to the presence of a professional killer.* This is an easy one to debunk. A murder is committed on television and the victim has his or her neck cleanly fractured. Or, perhaps, a body is discovered with a single bullet hole to the side of the head (sometimes after being double-tapped to the heart). The assassin might as well place a note on the body "Death by John Q. Assassin, Esquire). The *first* thing that a professional killer wants to do is to place space – time *and* distance – between themselves and the scene of the crime. The only way that they can achieve this effectively is to disguise the killings as either accidental or, perhaps, routine. Anything else and the police will secure every airport, train station, bus depot, and hotel for a hundred miles or more in every direction.

This represents the fundamental purpose of this book. Not to teach you how to employ yourself as a professional killer; rather, how to distinguish truth from fantasy, practicality from absurdity. You cannot defend yourself against myths. You cannot apprehend fables. Assassins are people – calculating, manipulative, innovative, and lethal as all hell – but people nevertheless. They are not supermen.

Home Away From "Wherever".

Safe houses remain death traps if they do not function properly. We employ the term "safe house" here for its traditional and ubiquitous meaning. In reality, however, we are discussing *safe havens*, an environment specially prepared by the professional killer to hide within, retrieve "bug out" supplies from, and/or locate operational necessities required for any period existing before, during, or after the assassination. These environments might be an actual house, a rented apartment or hotel room, a ship or yacht, an aircraft, an abandoned industrial building, a jungle hideaway, or a plot of land in the middle of the desert.

What makes the safe haven unique amongst all the other provisions of the assassination business, is that it cannot be traced back to ownership of the killer. Virtually everything else employed – including those offshore bank accounts and bearer-certificate-owned corporations "can" be traced back to the assassin should sufficient manpower and time be available for the law enforcement community. Safe houses are not owned directly by the assassin or via any institution owned by that particular individual. Some simply represent apartments rented under false identities (many landlords, especially those on the fringe of the community, only care about the cash they receive. This is particularly true with many furnished motels that offer weekly rates).

Another function of safe havens remains the concept of "get out of jail" materials. That is, no self-respecting professional assassin is going to survive very long without "something" in place should he or she be captured or even targeted for killing themselves. As dwellers of the lower rungs of human depravity, assassins bear an intimate understanding of how corporations, governments, and even militaries work. This leaves them privy to all sorts of compromising data that can serve to keep him or her alive and out of danger as effectively as possible. Knowing, say, that a particular assassin bears biological or chemical weapons secreted within a half dozen or more cities may keep the indigenous law enforcement community eternally gazing the other way.

Or, perhaps, he or she bears compromising data on numerous business executives, labor leaders, politicians, etc. that *will* come to the public should anything "unfortunate" ever happen to that particular individual. Such national leaders may seek to protect the assassin less this information suddenly appear on the desk of hundreds of journalists and media organizations. The professional assassin remains, eternally, a *prepared* individual and no one understands the lengths that he or she will go through to affect their trade. As with any animal in nature, they can become quite *vicious* when cornered or threatened. Some feel that it is best to leave them alone.

Still, the conscientious killer is not an indiscriminate killer, which is why they generally do not employ terroristic methods of assassination.[34] When they do employ such methods, it remains only because causing small-scale panic (think of the Robert F. Kennedy or, possibly, John F. Kennedy assassinations) permits them to extract themselves from an otherwise enclosed assassination target. However, these should be considered the very remote exceptions to the rule. Again, assassins do not live very long if they make it a routine to conduct their trade within a closed environment.

Safe havens permit the professional killer to avoid retracing his steps after conducting an assassination by existing as a prearranged (and largely uncontaminated) destination where

---

[34] According to the ~1950s CIA assassination manual "A Study of Assassination", terroristic assassinations represent those that require publicity to be effective. The professional assassin, to the contrary, rarely seeks publicity of the sort that would panic the population.

appearances can be altered, travel arrangements documented, or covers can be authenticated. Alternatively, an assassin may use a safe house to simply wait out the expected law enforcement response before she calmly relocates to another city or country.

Safe havens, by virtue of their intended function, must adhere to the following requirements:

> 1. The safe haven must be uncompromised and isolated from the assassin;
>
> 2. The safe haven must be located at a site far enough away from the assassination to ensure that it remains outside immediate law enforcement scrutiny and yet close enough that the killer can reach the site before large-scale police response blocks escape and evasion routes;
>
> 3. The safe haven must permit either a change in cover or appearance of the assassin without compromising the mission (e.g., an assassin changing into a janitor cover cannot operate out of a high end residence);
>
> 4. The safe haven must allow for abandonment without raising suspicions should the assassin decide that it has been compromised (e.g., weekly rentals of a motel room can be dropped without raising suspicion from the owner or manager).

As for the benefits of various types of safe havens, the following chart categorizes the merits of each individual option according to Expediency, Confidentiality, Affordability, and Liquidity. That is, which option bears merits as to how quickly the safe haven can be reached, how secure the option remains in light of progressive police response following an assassination, how affordable the site remains (understanding that assassins are likely to employ numerous sites around the world), and how quickly the safe haven can be disposed of once its use is no longer needed (darker shades representing higher ratings).

	Expediency	Confidentiality	Affordability	Liquidity
House		10		
Motel (Weekly)		7		
Maritime Vessel		9		
Abandoned Structure		1		
Remote Camp		5		
Vehicular Hide.		<1		

Each of these options remains generalized for the purposes of discussion. For instance, a motor yacht for a city on the coast may score higher in the Expediency department than would a detached house. Similarly, a remote camp in the jungle or desert would, obviously, score higher than a vehicular hide. This illustrates a mere portion of the pre-planning phase that a professional killer must consider before he or she even agrees to accept the contract. The numbers under the Confidentiality category represent an indication of how long each option could be expected to retain such a condition. For example, a higher number indicates that the assassin can reside within that safe haven for a longer period before being compromised by a search, neighbors, or unforeseen circumstances.

More important than mere hides, however, remains the concept of secured communications, without which no assassin could effectively operate. Such communications represent the *only* link between the assassin and the client, between the assassin's mind and the assassination itself.

Defeating Ears and Eyes.

It remains nearly impossible to communicate with others without leaving a trace of your voice or words for others to retrieve at will. If you were someone whose job necessitated the murder of another human being, however, particularly one that required an ability to escape apprehension and prosecution, you would be expected to avoid these trappings of modern communications as well. No need to worry, however, for every opportunity to communicate bears an equally strong opportunity to disguise one's words.

The first step in avoiding compromising discussions rests with compartmentalizing private communications from the myriad of activities that associate a particular individual with his or her thoughts and actions. Pre-paid cell phones and messages 'left in draft' on shared email accounts work well for terrorists and other criminals, but professional assassins do not operate in groups. Such individuals require more complex methods of communication (with whom shall be left to the reader's imagination).

Two solutions (and possibly combinations of them) avail themselves to the professional assassin:

- **Steganography**. The tactic of embedding files within other files such as "graphics, sound, text, HTML, and PDF" files today, has been around since 580 B.C.;[35]

- **One-Time Pad**. Invented in 1917 by Maj. Joseph Mauborgne and Gilbert Vernam of AT&T, the one-time pad still rates as the world's only "perfect encryption

---

[35] Andy Jones, Gerald L. Kovacich, and Perry G. Luzwick *Global Information Warfare: How Businesses, Governments, and Others Achieve Objectives and Attain Competitive Advantages* (Boca Raton, FL: Auerbach Publications, 2002), 48-49.

scheme."[36]Its encryption comes solely from like-pads, which are disposed of once the message is deciphered and a new key is used for future messages. Assuming that either pad is not compromised, messages are secure and free from interference.

A very secure communications between an assassin and his or her client may represent something like this:

> A client posts an innocuous PDF file on the Internet (concerning, say, entomology) and on page 36 of the document is an image of an innocent house fly. The assassin, knowing of the document beforehand, also understands that the photograph of the housefly (*Musca domestica*) is unusual because the presence of an "ordinary" housefly within a much more specialized research document pegs his interest more than would any other reader. Beneath the image rests a link to a larger photograph of the "innocent" housefly and the assassin downloads the image onto his computer. Afterwards, he uses a steganography software program to retrieve an embedded file from the image containing details regarding the target.

Or

> An assassin maintains a membership profile on an international dating site. He is looking for a "particular" woman who contacts him under the pretense of seeking a husband. He reads the woman's profile and observes certain 'identifiers' that suggest communication from a potential client. The assassin then replies to the women's correspondence with carefully selected words and phrases. On a pre-determined date, a reply is had along with five (an agreed to number) photographs and a short description of each. The assassin, by reputation, understands which photograph should be decrypted through the steganography program and extracts the contract information from the image.

---

[36] Bruce Schneier, *Applied Cryptography, Second Edition* (New York: John Wiley & Sons, 1996), 15.

Neither of these avenues actually represent secured communications simply because the dozens or hundreds of people viewing the same material bear no idea of the hidden messages contained within the photographs. With the billions upon billions of files and communications available via the Internet, there remains no sure way of scrutinizing *everything* that flows through cyberspace. Furthermore, neither of the above two examples warrant compromising messages stored within the "draft folder" of a shared email account that could reveal the identity of at least one party.

The second option is even more enticing as it allows clients to share reputations of various assassins without sacrificing the identity of any particular individual. A professional may, for instance, scour various dating sites for, say, a 26-year-old, 5'6" blond named Anna, who enjoys crocheting and racquetball. The assassin understands that such an individual *may* represent a client and a few brief communications will either confirm or deny the contact. If not, he simply ceases communication with the woman and follows all other leads. Even in the wide world of Internet dating, the particulars of the "one" profile are arranged so that misconceptions remain negligible.

Unlike the various intelligence and espionage agencies, the assassin-client relationship does not offer any chance of face-to-face encounters. If you are forking over a million or two to silence a business competitor or remove a security threat to your family, the *last thing you want is to be photographed with an assassin.* Intelligence agencies violate this rule all of the time, which probably explains why terrorists and transnational criminal organizations (TCO) operate so effectively all around the world. During the height of the Cold War, for example, the British utilized the *wife of the MI6 Moscow station chief to meet with a Russian agent!*[37]Can you say "stupid" boys and girls?

If, in the exceedingly rare event, that an assassin must meet with an individual (never the client or anyone associated with the client), say to retrieve critical supplies or tools, then a dead drop is used. A slight mark is made in chalk at a predetermined location or, perhaps, an individual walks innocently by the assassin with a "peculiar kink" in his shoelaces announcing that a drop had been made at a predetermined cache point. No words are spoken. No messages left in text. And, in the case of the strange shoelaces, no one *ever* notices someone making a mark upon a wall in chalk for no apparent reason.

The rule of thumb here is to avoid *all detectable communications* between the assassin and other individuals. In an age where individuals cannot drive an automobile without having to send a text message describing the activity, communicant avoidance seems absurd. Nevertheless, communications via the Internet or cellular towers leave data behind that can compromise many covert activities. For this reason, the use of such technologies must involve encryption and unbreakable codes. The "messages" are not live feeds, but rather *deposited* nuggets of data that even if they could be found, would take months and years to decipher.

If an assassin's communications are minimal, his or her movements are not. Perhaps more so than nearly any other individual, the professional killer remains constantly on the move, accepting new assignments and broadening distance (both physical and evidentiary) from past missions. Communications represent a very insignificant portion of the

---

[37] Victor Cherkashin and Gregory Feifer, *Spy Handler: Memoir of a KGB Officer: The True Story of the Man Who Recruited Robert Hanssen & Aldrich Ames* (New York: Basic Books, 2005), 66.

job, ultimately revolving around target acceptance and payment. The client "knows" when the contract has been completed and the assassin receives the final payment upon completion. In a world where many cannot make the simplest decision without conferring with dozens of friends, the assassin-client relationship remains exceedingly brief. Certainly not extensive enough to fashion a television show or motion picture about. More significant, however, remains the assassin's plans for travel and evasion.

Escape & Evasion.

For an individual constantly on the move (though not necessarily *consistently moving*) plans must be in place to transit territory or vacate safe havens within a minute's notice. Humans are not as fixed and rigid as they appear. Some individuals have relocated thousands of miles across the United States with little more than a suitcase and a bus ticket or have ventured down to South America for several weeks with only $20 to their name.[38]Therefore, it does not represent any extraordinary ability for a trained and prepared individual, such as a professional killer, to leave on a minute's notice and reappear halfway around the planet with no plans to come back to their former hide.

Escape & Evasion (E&E), for the assassin, represents little more than a planned itinerary with provisions for Murphy's Law included. That is, "escape" represents a very rare tactic for the killer and "evasion" simply a code of practice. Being a professional, however, requires one to be prepared for every eventuality and since assassinations represent human endeavors – consisting of both victims and bystanders – things *can* go awry. The victim may ultimately not "cooperate" (perhaps that allergy to peanuts was largely psychosomatic) or

---

[38] Memorandum for the record, R.J. Godlewski.

68

bystander behavior foils the assassin's previously well-orchestrated plans. In either case, rare as it may be, the assassin must vacate the location and proceed towards a safe haven to attempt another strike at a later date.

The first concern involves, naturally, a method of transportation. Assassins often are depicted hurrying away from the scene of the murder via a motorcycle. This remains problematic, however. A motorcycle whisking away in crowded traffic or down a dark alley tends to be noticed, even within the city. Similarly, wearing full body leather (as is often depicted) further identifies the assassin as "unusual" and driving a motorcycle while wearing a suit and tie may be impractical.

A better option for escape from the scene of the assassination (assuming that secondary conveyance is warranted) is to have another automobile parked nearby. A nondescript car parked along, say, a street on which any number of vehicles are parked will not arouse interest unless a neighbor or security agent has memorized all the local vehicles. The assassin could park such a vehicle on the day before the assassination, drive into the location with one vehicle (properly sanitized), conduct the killing, and then vacate the area via another vehicle. This obviously increases the complexity of the operation, but remains more subdued than roaring away on a motorcycle.

Professional assassinations represent a business – a bloody, diabolical, and emotionless business, but a business just the same – and therefore the romanticism and intrigue of Hollywood movies simply do not take place (even heroic war stories are doctored for effect). Most assassinations occur with the killer simply walking away from the scene of the crime as if nothing happened. Dashing away to "safety" illustrates the presence of an amateur or a killer employing terroristic assassination methods. Running away, therefore, bears all the hallmarks of a snatch-and-grab jewelry store or bank robber. When a crime has been committed, the *first* person people look at is the one bolting helter-skelter away from the scene.

If there remains one aspect that *all* professional assassins share, it is *confidence.* Confident professionals simply do not panic. Professional football quarterbacks do not lose composure on fourth down with the ball on the twenty-yard line and seconds left on the clock. Professional baseball pitchers do not become unglued with the bases loaded at the bottom of the ninth inning of a tied World Series game. Professional police marksmen do not become nervous when a crazed killer is holding a pistol to the head of a hostage. Professionals remain those who can be counted upon to do their "thing" day in and day out and professional assassins are not an exception to the rule.

Their egress from the scene of the crime is as well planned (if not more so) as any other facet of the mission for which he or she had planned for weeks or months. The assassin's movements are coordinated, choreographed, disciplined, and efficient. Their movements from the scene of the attack, whether it represents a shooting within a crowded room or having had doped the victim's martini, does not arouse suspicion from those surrounding them. This is key; an assassin *can* run away from the center of crisis if *everyone* else is doing so too. To walk when others flee is to draw attention to oneself.

Consider the following scenarios:

> An assassin perched along a ridge looking down upon an expansive country estate takes down a victim horseback riding from long-range (1000+ meters – an *exceptional* assassination mission) with a rifle that can be broken down into its constituent components. Upon placing the shot, the assassin calmly disassembles the rifle, places the weapon components into a bag and hauls the bag high up into a tree

utilizing a clear monofilament, 30-pound test fishing line that had been previously secreted for the mission. Once the bag is *locked* into position via a one-way pulley, the fishing line is secured against the tree where it becomes unnoticed to anyone not actually inspecting the specific tree. The assassin then retrieves another bag that contains a camera bearing numerous photographs of nearby sights and calmly proceeds to the location of the photography, climbs into a 4x4 Toyota FJ Cruiser (replete with various accessories of a nature photographer) and calmly drives away *towards* the direction from where police and emergency medical personnel are expected to appear.

Alternatively,

An assassin has just 'tripped' a lone victim down a flight of stairs at an apartment building using a piece of heavy twine that had been looped around a stanchion. Once the fall had commenced, the killer simply recovers the twine rapidly and passes the ball of string into his pocket as he simultaneously lends "aid" to victim, ensuring that the job had reached its intended consequences. Once it had been determined that the victim's neck had been broken, the "innocent witness" calls out for "someone" to call for an ambulance. As a crowd gathers to the scene of the accident, the assassin simply retreats towards the back of the group, perhaps feigning nervousness over the "lack of medical knowledge" (assassins *know* medical procedures). Even when the ambulance arrives (the police may or may not show), the municipal procedure remains for the "authorities" to take over the situation and, at worst, the assassin simply needs to make an "everything happened so fast" statement and then calmly walk out of the building and board the nearest bus to relocate to where a car is waiting for a more extended trip out of the area

The two scenarios outlined above are simplistic to prove a point – this book is *not* intended to teach you how to become a professional assassin – and that point remains to understand that neither assassination involves the killer dashing out of the location, hurdling the hoods of cars in the process, with the police in hot pursuit.[39] In fact, in the second scenario the police may not arrive at all and then only because they happened to be in the area and *may* have to serve some public function as to notify next of kin or record the scene for insurance purposes. With the string quickly tossed into some distant trash receptacle, there probably is not sufficient evidence for the police to employ the services of already stretched criminal investigative teams. People fall all of the time, some even die within the process.

An assassin's departure from the scene of a crime, whether by bicycle or automobile, usually follows a pattern. First, the killer leaves the immediate scene by way of appropriate indigenous transport (e.g., a local bus in a major city, a car in the suburbs, a motorcycle or all-terrain vehicle in the desert, etc.). Once the assassin relocates out of the "hot zone" – the immediate area where response efforts are likely to materialize – he or she then transfers to a more practical vehicle of opportunity (say, a train in Europe or Asia, a ship in Oceania, etc.) Finally, the assassin leaves the nation aboard aircraft or ship for a (generally) destination that is likely to complicate extradition back to where the murder occurred.

Particularly with "major" assassinations that are likely to influence law enforcement response, the professional killer "flips the coin" by traveling to the opposite side of the planet as far away from the crime as possible. This is *not* to say that an individual simply shoots J.D. Moneybags in New York City and then hops aboard a commercial airliner flying to Singapore. On the contrary. The assassin may, indeed, be heading towards Singapore, but he or she is likely to take the "scenic route" there and engage several days or even an entire week or more before they reach their final safe haven of choice.

---

[39] Even "hot pursuits" are diminishing today as cities and local governments come under increasing scrutiny for endangering the public within high-speed chases along the freeways.

New York to Singapore "Escape"

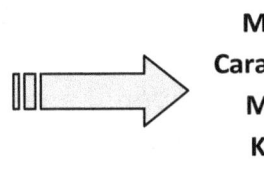

New York City	San Juan, Puerto Rico
San Juan, Puerto Rico	Miami, Florida
Miami, Florida	Caracas, Venezuela
Caracas, Venezuela	Madrid, Spain
Madrid, Spain	Kiev, Ukraine
Kiev, Ukraine	Singapore

The assassin flees New York City, spends three days in San Juan before returning to the U.S. to spend one day in Miami. He then flies down to Caracas for two days before flying up to Madrid for three days. From Madrid, he travels to Kiev for three days before catching a flight to Singapore.

Added to the above scenario could be any number of "facets" designed to disrupt potential pursuers, such as living aboard a sailing yacht in San Juan, driving down to Crimea from Kiev before returning to the Ukrainian capital, or simply catching earlier flights than those originally booked. Once in Singapore, the assassin could remain for an extended period or begin to immediately travel back to the United States or other destination of choice through ship, aircraft, or motor yacht.

The "Evasion" portion of the trip simply involves the myriad of possibilities designed to distract observing authorities. This includes booking conflicting flights, altering hotel accommodations, and changing identities as permissible. The less "drastic" the assassination, the less "disruptive" the escape and evasion plan (which probably explains why Hollywood movies are more action-adventure than bland recitations of murder theory).

A fundamental part of any assassination plan rests the E&E cache, or what those within the personal security field would refer to as a "bug out" bag or kit. This simply represents a (normally) 72-hour supply of whatever the individual may need to handle an unforeseen crisis. The difference with the professional assassin, however, remains that this particular "crisis" is known and experienced. Therefore, he or she retains a E&E cache at all safe havens, each tailored towards a specific function (usually designed to survive within the indigenous location for a few days and to permit relocation to another safe haven).

In the above New York City to Singapore scenario, the E&E bag in San Juan, for instance, would include locally purchased souvenirs to which are added, say, newspapers acquired during a period of time prior to the assassination in New York (which could authenticate a cover that the assassin had been vacationing in Puerto Rico for the duration). The E&E kit in Caracas, to the contrary, may possess counterfeit Spanish credentials permitting the assassin to "return" to Madrid as a Spanish citizen.

No assassin can function discreetly or professionally without an escape plan, fortified with the necessary supplies and cover identities that *may* be required if the mission did not go according to plan. Most of this involves the broad range of time that he or she works *between* assassination assignments, shoring investments, developing indigenous resources, and adapting to "adoptive" cultures.

7

HUMAN DEATH...AND KILLING HUMANS: THE LIVELIHOOD OF THE ASSASSIN.

Contrary to popular expectations, the death of human beings remains a very time-consuming, physiological function. For instance, a person suffering from the complications associated with cancer or Alzheimer's disease may take several days to progress through the "passing" phase of death.[40] More instantaneous forms of death – *killing* – can only come by way of intense accidental or malicious human intervention.

It remains this "artificial" method that serves as the assassin's stock and trade. No other human occupation rests more devoted to facilitating death than the professional killer. Not the police. Not the military. Not even gang, terrorist, or Mafia hit squads serve death *exclusively*. Within the next

---

[40] Memorandum for the record, R.J. Godlewski. 2003, 2008.

chapter, we shall discuss both governmental (Central Intelligence Agency) and terrorist (al-Qaeda) assassination programs and how they specifically divert from the concept of the individual, professional killer. Excerpts from both the CIA and Jihadist assassination "manuals" will be used to distinguish bureaucratic killing from its more capitalistic version (professional killers murder *exclusively* for monetary gain, despite some element of idealism within their target selection). Death, however, remains far more indiscriminate; *everyone* dies eventually.

Death, perhaps like pornography, remains decidedly difficult to define, yet everyone recognizes it whenever they see it. Colloquially speaking, death represents the ceasing of biological functions within the human body, most notably that involving cerebral control of the circulatory and respiratory systems. Humans have held a ritual fascination with deliberately and honorably burying the dead for at least 23,000 years, adorning their passed companions with jewelry and clothing.[41]Those individuals viewed as having died bravely within wars and other heroic actions often have received even greater care in their burial and remembrance.

The care and dedication with which the ancients honored their dead serves to illustrate the fundamental value that humanity placed upon life in general. For more than 2,000 years, the Christian ethic had been that human life remained so infinitely valuable, that the greatest love one could show was to lay down his or her life for their neighbors.[42]For as long, the Roman Catholic Church has declared:

"The deliberate murder of an innocent person is gravely

---

[41] Colin Renfrew and Paul Bahn, *Archaeology: Theories, Methods, and Practice, Third Edition* (New York: Thames & Hudson, 2000), 389.

[42] See John 13:13 *New American Bible*: "No one has greater love than this, to lay down one's life for one's friends."

contrary to the dignity of the human being, to the golden rule, and to the holiness of the Creator. The law forbidding it is universally valid: it obliges each and everyone, always and everywhere."[43]The indiscriminate and intentional killing of *any* human being rests forever outside the bounds of Western, civilized culture. For this very reason, the mere mentioning of the word "assassin" sends chills along the spine of ordinary individuals.

It is, perhaps, because the very word descended from a brutal and savage Islamist cult that, over the centuries, people have developed an innate fear of the word, a primal resentment of *anyone* serving killing exclusively. We do not fear gangs, criminals, even psychopaths in the same degree as "assassination" bears upon our soul. The various "what if?" questions lingering from the murders of Presidents Lincoln and Kennedy fuel and terrify the imagination. Yet, these represented one-off murders. One assailant was caught and died. The other, too, despite mounting evidence that the second murderer may not have acted alone.

Nevertheless, all humans remain, to a degree, obsessed with the prospects of death.[44] We try to cheat it, extend our precious lives through healthy eating and exercise. Others tempt fate innocuously through various role playing games including one virtual rendition of *Assassin's Creed*®. Only the truly ignorant and honestly incapacitated escape this fear of death. For the rest of humanity, it lingers as either a selfish barrier or a religious opportunity. Even the professional killer fears his or her own death, which is why they spend more of their time preparing on how to prolong their own lives than taking of the others'.

Because death comes, basically, through one of two avenues

---

[43] *Catechism of the Catholic Church* (New York: Bantam Doubleday, 1995), Paragraph #2261.
[44] Grossman, *On Killing*, 47.

– ceasing of the circulatory-respiratory system or extensive damage to the cerebrospinal pathways that guide electrical impulses from the brain to the various organs and muscles of the body – the outcome of the various "techniques" of the assassin remain rather limited. After all, a pillow held tightly to the face bears the same result as a room full of Sarin gas. Similarly, a tumble down the stairs affects much the same result as ten pounds of C4 explosive. Dead is dead.

What separates the professional assassin (defined as someone who carries out highly discriminate murders for pay) from other homicidal criminals (defined as anyone who carries out often indiscriminate murders, that may or may not include innocent bystanders, through order or for pay), is that the professional assassin tends to mask his or her actions as either *accidental* or (very rarely) the result of the action of a homicidal criminal. Part of this distinction rests with the fact that the assassin needs to *prove* the death of the target individual. Simply blowing up a high-rise apartment complex, for example, does little to authenticate the death of a particular individual. Humans have been known to escape the jaws of death from even the most horrific disasters.

To secure against this potentiality, the assassin normally allows "municipal authority" to pronounce the execution of the contract. That is, police reports, media statements, and the all-important obituary notice serve to announce the death of a target without further involvement of the assassin (which facilitates escape) or the client (which isolates him or her from interest within the murdered victim). Again, the assassin business remains a *business* – little more.

The most significant part of this enterprise, however, remains *getting away* with the murder in question. The assassin's business effectively ends – permanently – if he or she is connected to the crime and their reputation ends –

again, permanently – if his or her client becomes connected to the murder. Blowing up entire buildings and machine-gunning down targets remains a surefire way to attract attention from law enforcement and other authority figures. One need not be so drastic to be suspicious.

A cleanly fractured neck and a corresponding bruise around the chin rule out, for instance, a victim innocently falling down a flight of stairs. A broken brake line and an overly inebriated victim rules out a "freak" accident as the cause of death. A person who dies from Malayan pit viper (*Callaselasma rhodostoma*) poison in Nome, Alaska is definitely going to raise some questions. A bedroom ceiling peppered with body parts following an explosion will not suggest a natural gas line rupture. These all represent amateurish attempts to assassinate an individual and all leave behind powerful forensic evidence that will *ultimately* lead to the true killer. It may take 10, 20, or 30 years and longer, but *someday* the murderer will become known.

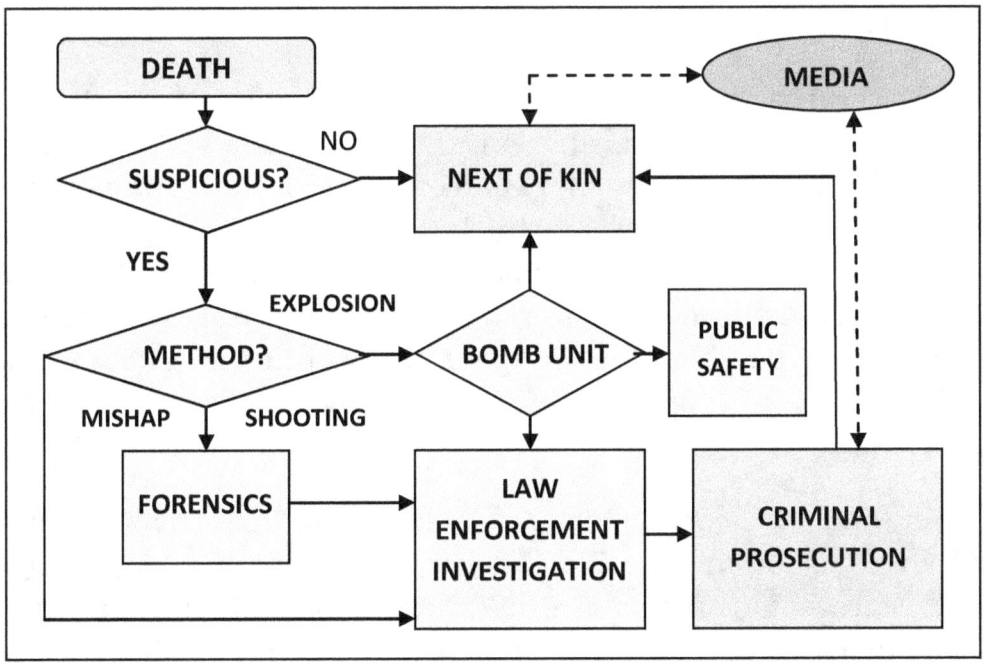

As the above graphic briefly implies, the professional assassin must navigate through a number of compromising scenarios in choosing his or her method of killing the victim. Any number of these "blocks" may, someday, come back to single out the perpetrator of the crime. Each method (shooting, accident, poisoning, fire, etc.) bears an infinite number of factors that can implicate – or, at a minimum, hinder – the assassin's mission of self-preservation. The appropriate method, therefore, remains of primary importance to the trade.

Never a Decision to Kill, but of How?

Whether or not to kill never enters the mind of an assassin. It remains simply *what* they do, inasmuch as any other member of society pursues his or her chosen profession with varying degrees of care. Unlike most, however, the professional assassin remains extremely dedicated to their function; as his or her life rests upon the ability to kill without being killed or apprehended. Death, for the assassin, remains little more than a science as well as an art. They cannot fathom the moral duplicity that most humans endure.

Discrimination in assignments rests largely with the practicality of the assassination. J.D. Moneybags may present a far easier target than, say, His Highness, King Dupries of the Wildebeests. Even if the money for the life of an emperor were extremely tempting, the assassin knows instinctively that such killings are "retirement" murders – meaning that the assassin would never be able to work again and would very likely spend the rest of his or her life constantly looking over their shoulders.

Yet, like pure contractors everywhere else, the assassin must kill in order to pay the bills and survive the intervening months and years before the next profitable contract. Therefore, there will *always* be business executives, political opponents, and despotic military leaders that will cease life on earth through

80

various methods of "mystery" that, at best, only two people on the planet bear knowledge of. True, there will be equally mysterious – if not fully unexplained – deaths of estranged (and violent) husbands, gang members, and rival Mafiosi, but these generally do not pay as well as to attract the attention of the *true professional* killer.

Even before accepting a contract, the assassin must consider *how* the target is likely to meet an unexpected end. Any death must appear "natural", otherwise foul play will be expected immediately. Let us reengage the equestrian scenario presented on pages 70 and 71. Instead, would it not have been better for the victim to have been thrown from the horse? Numerous people are injured and killed within horseback riding accidents every year, making the equestrian sports some of the most dangerous in the world. Even if the victim is not killed outright from the fall, he may be laid up within the hospital offering an opportunity for the assassin to finish them off later under the auspices of medical "complications".

The foregoing death may not be as instantaneous, but the results would not be scrutinized as much either. The problem for the assassin, however, remains the tradeoff between quick and verifiable death and an aspect of plausible deniability. Then, *how*, exactly, would an assassin cause a horse to throw its rider off in a manner sufficiently violent enough to bear a chance of mortally wounding the rider? Much would depend upon the intelligence that the assassin learned about the victim. Perhaps the victim bore a habit of drinking too much before his evening rides. If the rider rode alone, a loud noise could provide enough of a jolt to startle the horse, perhaps throwing the rider down a small ravine.

The quickest form of death results from the incapacitation of the brain to perform the required bodily functions necessary to sustain life. The neck snaps, the brain is cut off from the heart and the lungs, and eventually the person "drains" away. How long this passing actually takes involves numerous variables and is best left for medical personnel and theologians to debate. The issue for the assassin rests with the breakage of the spinal cord itself. If the break is *clean*, then it suggests a professional attack. On the other hand, how does an assassin assure an irregular break? The entirety of the conditions under which the assassin surveys the victim may rule out opportunities for such "casual" attacks.

If a 'neck break' scenario remains impossible, the assassin must consider another plausible way in which to terminate the target without raising suspicions. Analysis of the intended victim's medical history may offer some insight into whether, say, cardiac arrest or allergic reaction may occur. Most humans are allergic to *something*. Others are not as physically fit as they think they are. A wrong drink here or an exertion there and the victim may be just as dead as if their spine was literally snapped in half. An assassin, for one, understands that both of these situations avail themselves within the swimming pool.

Numerous drugs remain indecipherable within the conditions associated with drowning. This scenario appears more valuable than, say, attempting to rip someone's head off from behind. Allergic reactions while swimming can also lead to drowning and remain even harder to distinguish from natural – rather non-artificially produced – deaths while swimming. The key here, is to remember the art and science of assassination – death is the science and killing remains the art.

The Artistry of Assassination Science.

To adequately understand the concept of death requires an extensive library of texts, quite beyond the scope of this book. The infamous *A Study of Assassination* prepared by the CIA simply lists the techniques of the trade as manual killing,

82

accidents, drugs, edged weapons, blunt weapons, firearms (comprising the vast majority of the discussion), and explosives within its roughly twelve pages of 8.5x11" equivalent text. From what was released on July 12, 1995, the "CIA assassination manual" remains less of a study or even a manual than a few brief excerpts on killing (see next chapter).

Of the seven stated devices of killing listed by the CIA, we have already discussed problems with manual killing (bare-handed breaking of the neck, etc.), edged and blunt weapons, firearms, and explosives. This leaves drugs (worse) and accidents (best) as the most beneficial methods of assassination for the professional killer. So much for Hollywood theatrics. Nevertheless, the science of death offers many opportunities within each scenario.

Death by natural gas asphyxiation may obscure death by another toxic gas. Killing with a garrote remains a lot cleaner forensically than killing with a bowie knife. Few bother to realize the numerous idiosyncrasies of forced death, often assuming that death is a cut and dry proposition (such as the various anti-gun groups that believe in killer guns). Consider knives, for instance. Hollywood's example of killing by blade spans from the hip, posturing gangs of *West Side Story* to innumerable war movies where unlucky sentries largely in the form of non-credited actors have had their throats ripped out. In reality, if you are using a knife to "silence" someone, you had better employ a dagger-style blade and thrust it deeply into one of the victim's kidneys. The rest will solve itself (hint: the victim will *not* be able to scream, fight back, or even move).

Professional assassins represent, perhaps, the *only* surgical instrument on the field of human-on-human battle. They accept a contract to kill *only* one person and then commit weeks, months, possibly even a year getting to know that particular individual before they design that specific person's death. Think about this for a moment. In a world where hundreds of thousands of people die every day from hunger, disease, injury, war, and crime, perhaps only one or two die from carefully articulated assassination. A great many more die from "targeted killings", but these necessarily involve the hostile actions of groups – either criminal or governmental in nature.

The subject of this book – the professional, contract assassin – remains the only individual that does not try to dispute their function. Soldiers serve governments and gang members often visualize their role as somehow being victimized by society in general. Even the Latin American drug cartels shield themselves from murder by saying something to the effect of, "Hey, if you had *only left us alone...*" It represents a dysfunction of humanity to realize how just many people actually kill and then blame someone else for the crime.

Perhaps this explains the abject fear that the rest of the human population experiences whenever they hear the mere word *assassin*. As a global population, we have grown accustomed to "wishing away" murderous despots into exile. They may have murdered tens or even hundreds of thousands of people, but we will "ignore" their crimes if they would just leave their countries and go impose upon some other tyrannical regime. Catch an assassin, however, and we want to emulate the ancient Japanese whenever they caught a ninja – we want them burned alive in hot oil. Or at least given the chair.

Could this simply represent a hatred of their honesty? Does our mind gloss over mass killing but reel back in horror over the life of someone whose sole function remains to murder an individual they have just spent months coming to know? How can people do such things? Because, frankly, humans have *always* done such things. The parable of Cain and Abel, remember, is that as long as two people are around – even if blood relatives – one bears the capability of killing the other.[45] Dr. Stanley Milgram of Yale University proved decades ago that 65% of the human population could be induced into killing another innocent individual.[46]The assassin simply holds no pretense about it.

Maybe individuals simply envy assassins. Again, *everyone* bears a mental list of people who they fantasize about harming, even if in passing moments. It remains as natural as fantasizing about marrying a popular movie star or model or actually winning the lottery for a change. The "artistry" of assassination remains that the professional killer works all of this into his or her routine. Assassins do not stand out because they know humanity far too well. They can literally get away with murder because, as true disciples of Sun-tzu, they know both themselves and their enemies intimately.

Those who fantasize about killing others do not "plan" on getting away with the crime because, obviously, they would never actually carry out the deed. Therefore, their visions of death involve beating the poor sap into a pulp, running them over with the family sedan, and, perhaps, nuking them and their entire family back into the Stone Age. Instead, people take out their frustrations on the football field, run marathons, and eat to excess. There remains far more people, sadly, who abuse their spouses and children than assassinate others leading, perhaps, to a growing list of "fantasy murders" within innocent human minds.

Whatever one's occupation, those who approach that profession as if an artist bear the opportunity to excel at his or her career for a great many years without failure. Often, people look upon a successful person and say "He's an artist on the

---

[45] Genesis 4:8, *NAB*.

[46] Grossman, *On Killing*, 141.

pitcher's mound" or "She is 'gifted' in business". Michelangelo did not begin by painting his own crib anymore than Leonardo da Vinci began designing his. The life of the victim represents a three-dimensional puzzle for the assassin, comprised of numerous pieces some slightly more powerful than others.

The destruction or "removal" of a single piece to the puzzle may not necessarily affect the entire structure. For instance, everyone stubs his or her toes every now and then, but no major damage occurs from the incident. On the other hand, suppose such an injury emerged serious enough to affect the way the person walked. A professional assassin would notice the slight subtlety and perhaps – *perhaps* – factor it into a plot to 'trip' the victim down a flight of stairs. What exists as a mere annoyance for the victim and something unworthy of consideration for nearly everyone else becomes a potential force-multiplier for the assassin.

Few citizens, for instance, can appreciate the effects of a remote-triggered airbag within a car. Or of the deaths caused by unintentional electrocution. No one, it can be argued, adequately reads the warning labels on various over-the-counter medicines. What motorist understands the intrinsic programming of an automobile's electronic throttle? Fashioning someone's untimely death and leaving the scene safely to commit another murder time after time does not require very much science. It remains, above all else, a human art.

8

ANNOTATED EXCERPTS FROM THE CIA AND AL-QAEDA ASSASSINATION MANUALS.

Although the professional assassin represents an independent contractor, freed from the corralling nature of bureaucracies through innovation and individualistic expediency, much can be learned from those organizations that employ killers on a broader level. These groups send out their assassins in teams, some comprising quasi-military special units trained to act in unison and even coordinate with others. Two of these organizations bear scrutiny within the study of *individual* professional killers. The U.S. Central Intelligence Agency (CIA) comes first and has largely been restricted from the use of assassination as a tool since the 1970s. The other group remains al-Qaeda, the now ideological, all-encompassing name affixed to any number of jihadist individuals and groups that support the beliefs of the late Osama Bin Laden.

As the first to be discussed is the CIA, its *A Study of Assassination* flows from Agency files involving its destabilization program in Guatemala circa ~1952. The second document represents the infamous "Manchester Manual" discovered by police in the United Kingdom and prepared under the auspices of al-Qaeda's *Military Studies in the Jihad Against the Tyrants*. The latter remains significantly lengthier than the CIA manual and offers numerous examples of assassination case studies – both successful and unsuccessful – and appears more of a military training document than, say, the guidelines offered by the Agency program.

Both of these documents will be discussed in truncated, excerpted form because they exceed the merits required by the individual, professional assassin. Annotations will bear this in mind and excuse the reader from delving into either document, which are available online.[47] Both of these programs imply centralized, organizational control of assassins and almost exclusive involve some form of terroristic assassination. The dichotomy between the professional assassin and bureaucratic killers will become, hopefully, more apparent.

A Study of Assassination (Central Intelligence Agency).

"When the decision to assassinate has been reached, the tactics of the operation must be planned, based upon an estimate of the situation similar to that used in military operations. The preliminary estimate will reveal gaps in information and possibly indicate a need for special equipment which must be procured or constructed. When all necessary data has been collected, an effective tactical plan can be prepared. All planning must be mental; no papers should ever contain evidence of the operation."

---

[47] http://rjgodlewski.com/CIAAssassinationManual.pdf;
http://rjgodlewski.com/TheAQManualManchester.pdf.

After beginning with a discussion of the various classifications of assassination (open, secret, terroristic, etc.), the Agency document shifts into more practical considerations. An assassination must be dealt with in the tactical mind, for the objective may be fleeting and protected. Intelligence regarding the targeted victim remains mandatory and reveals strengths to avoid and weaknesses to exploit. The "special equipment" procured or constructed could be as simple as that heretofore pulley rig to hide a rifle broken down into a bag or as complex as an assassination weapon itself. Most of all, however, remains the need to keep any and all planning mental. *Under no circumstances would the professional assassin commit any operational data to written or digital format.*

> *"The essential point of assassination is the death of the subject. A human being may be killed in many ways but sureness is often overlooked by those who may be emotionally unstrung by the seriousness of this act they intend to commit. The specific technique employed will depend upon a large number of variables, but should be constant in one point: Death must be absolutely certain."*

Unlike the "drive-by" murders of gangs and narcotics cartels, the professional assassin remains constricted by the no cure-no pay contract that he or she agrees to. In this sense, they are not going to spray a house with an AK-47 anymore than they are going to detonate a vehicular bomb near a high-rise apartment building. In all likelihood, the assassin will actually watch the life literally drain out of the victim's eyes before they venture away from the scene of the crime. Or, at a minimum, they will quickly check for a pulse and then wait for the authorities to confirm the hit. Regardless, the assassin works within "close quarters killing" mode as much as possible; few are willing to forego the fee by taking chances.

"For secret assassination, either simple or chase, the contrived accident is the most effective technique. When successfully executed, it causes little excitement and is only casually investigated."

The CIA discussion comes after the employment of manual techniques, such as bare hands (which the Agency author correctly considers as too problematic), and hammers, axes, screw drivers, wrenches, etc. In "accidents", the manual primarily discusses falls of at least 75 feet onto hard surfaces and recommends elevator shafts, stair wells, unscreened windows, and bridges (though bridges over water should be avoided due to the unreliability of landing upon water). Many of these suggestions probably worked better in 1954 than during 2012, but falls are falls and, after properly considering the omnipresence of security cameras, falls down stairs or even "drunks" laying upon busy railroad tracks still serve their intended purpose.

In the "Drugs" second, the best advice provided by the Agency author is that morphine injected as a heavy drinker passes out will cause death attributable to alcoholism. Discussions on edged, blunt, and firearms weapons remain a bit more in-depth, though unreliability remains the fundamental consideration. In 2012 and beyond, both blunt weapons (baseball bats, rocks, etc.) and firearms furnish far too much forensic evidence to remain safe. Hence, the assassin-shooter of the 21st century is likely to use a shotgun at close range or a sabot rifle round at longer range to disrupt CSI-intensive communities. If the assassination occurs within a Third World environment then, perhaps, less efforts are required (understanding that "eventually" everyone catches up with advanced technologies).

Contrasting with Hollywood, the Agency manual questions the viability of suppressed weaponry, such as a pistol that "combines the disadvantages of any pistol with the added one of its obviously clandestine purpose." In the era of the manual, suppressors (a.k.a., "silencers") were definitely illegal. In 2012 America, most states permit suppressors (subject to federal licensing and fees) so they have gained a measure of respectability for sportsmen and gun enthusiasts.

One final statement regarding firearms is worth mentioning :

> **"A telescopically sighted, closed-action carbine shooting a low velocity bullet of great weight, and built for accuracy, could be very useful to an assassin in certain situations. At the time of writing, no such weapon is known to exist."**

Today, several manufacturers have developed excellent firearms that meet these requirements.

> *"The major factor which affects reliability is the use of explosives for assassination. The charge must be very large and the detonation must be controlled exactly as to time by the assassin who can observe the subject. A small or moderate explosive charge is highly unreliable as a cause of death, and time delay or booby-trap devices are extremely prone to kill the wrong man. In addition to the moral aspects of indiscriminate killing, the death of casual bystanders can often produce public relations unfavorable to the cause for which the assassination is carried out."*

Obviously, the Agency document argues against the use of explosives by the professional assassin working his or her "no cure-no pay" contract. No "professional" assassin wants to kill indiscriminately or chance a recovery of the victim. In a strange suggestion for assassination of any kind, the CIA devotes a rather large paragraph discussing that at least "ten pounds of high explosive should normally be regarded as a minimum"

91

and even discussing mortar shells ranging from 81mm to 120mm and antipersonnel artillery shells from 85mm to 105mm howitzers as advisable instruments of destruction.

Such improvised explosive devices (IEDs) are notorious within Afghanistan, Iraq, and the greater Middle East/Northern Africa (MENA) region, but remain questionable as a broad option for *professional* assassination. The function of a skilled assassin, remember, is to kill a *selected* target and avoid compromising all involved within the assassination. To literally get away with murder, a professional killer *must* disguise the attack as anything *but* a targeted killing. A 120mm mortar shell going off in, say, Chicago is not going to go unnoticed. Shrapnel will flood the streets and all that it would take is for one small child to receive injuries and all hell will break lose. Even if the assassin were trying to "disguise" the attack by blaming someone else, such an excessive use of explosives will very likely end that particular assassin's career.

The CIA, it must be remembered, during the 1950s when *A Study of Assassination* was written literally controlled all limited wars undertaken by the United States. The Agency wanted to defeat all communist infiltration into the Western Hemisphere and teaching Latin Americans how to use artillery shells to kill remained no different than al-Qaeda today using daisy-chained artillery shells to defeat all Western infiltration into the East.

Declaration of Jihad Against The Country's Tyrants (Al Qaeda MILITARY SERIES)

"Islamic governments have never and will never be established through peaceful solutions and cooperative councils. They are established as they always have been by pen and gun, by word and bullet, by tongue and teeth."

The al-Qaeda "Manchester Manual" is *not* for the

fainthearted. It begins with a declaration that peace is most assuredly *not* part of Jihadists' game plan nor is diplomacy an accepted tool. The distinction here with everything else covered within this book, is that al-Qaeda, Hezbollah, HAMAS, the Muslim Brotherhood, and all other Islamist/Jihadist organizations could care less about discriminate killing. They seek assassination solely for its *terroristic* appeal.

The al-Qaeda manual – effectively a *true* military style training manual – begins, as could be expected, with several pages of verses from the Quran and Hadith, as well as other religiously-tone accusations against "non-believers" and the non-Muslim world. The fighters of al-Qaeda represent religious terrorists and any assassinations carried out by them are done for Allah, Muhammad, and Islam. No profit but Prophet, in other words. This dichotomy sets them apart from the professional assassin and the manual's "first lesson" is largely a repetition of military organization, structure, and the need for intelligence in order to facilitate "overthrow of the godless regimes and their replacement with an Islamic regime."

> "It is well known that in undercover operations, communication is the mainstay of the movement for rapid accomplishment. However, it is a doubled-edged sword: It can be to our advantage if we use it well and it can be a knife dug into our back if we do not consider and take the necessary security measures."

The al-Qaeda operative remains, beyond anything else, a member of a broader cause. Even small, "lone wolf" cells must communicate with someone else to achieve their goals, even if that "someone else" is simply a religious advisor. The professional assassin, conversely, does not see communications as a "double-edged" sword; he or she sees *any* communication as a clear and present danger to their existence and, even when using one-time pads or steganography, kept to the absolute minimum. Al-Qaeda, however, remains a militant jihadist element and, much like the Ku Klux Klan within the United States, requires organizational instructions no matter how many fringes of the core organization compete for publicity. This reality is illustrated by the breadth of the security precautions the manual proposes surrounding group meetings.[48]

> *"The brother should draw a diagram of the area, the street, and the location which is the target of the information-gathering. He should describe its shape and characteristics. The drawing should be realistic so that someone who never saw the location could visualize it. It is preferable to also put on the drawing the directions of traffic, police stations, and security centers."*

The above represents just a small quotation from the manual discussing intelligence gathering. What it shows, is that al-Qaeda operatives are very appreciative of surveillance and reconnaissance. This parallels the requirements of the professional assassin with the significant exception that the professional does not reply upon *anyone else* to provide critical data regarding assassination missions – a very self-contained Intelligence, Surveillance, and Reconnaissance (ISR) operation.

> *"**Gather Information Through Interrogation**: Security personnel in our countries arrest brothers and obtain the needed information through interrogation and torture. The Military Organization must do likewise. On one hand, the Organization can obtain important information about enemy establishments and personnel. On the other hand, that is a form of necessary punishment."*

---

[48] The al-Qaeda manual approximates 140 pages in length – far too detailed to be recounted in entirety within this book – and the reader is encouraged to read the original document that covers far more than mere "assassinations". All editing herein by R.J. Godlewski.

That al-Qaeda and other Islamist elements physically torture people (not necessarily prisoners) goes without saying. The professional assassin does not interrogate through torture – it remains ineffective and compromises security – but must be aware of these conditions should he or she accept an assassination assignment in an Islamist country. Western-style agencies will never gain the intelligence that Muslim groups can obtain and the professional assassin will never possess the resources to emulate the Islamists. Interestingly, the al-Qaeda manual details the "kind of person" that the CIA seeks, perhaps a good lesson in counterintelligence.

Of value in studying the al-Qaeda document remains its broad appreciation and description of various cryptographic techniques for communication. Not of value to the communications reluctant assassin, these discussions could come in handle should the professional's ISR function come across enticing coded information. Even if not deciphered, such information can point to the existence of an al-Qaeda cell within the assassination environment (remember that "get out of jail" package, an assassin could make friends with certain knowledge about national enemies poised to attack entire cities).

When the al-Qaeda manual finally reaches the subject of assassination (along with kidnapping), it begins with an interesting history of firearms and the discussion of both pistol and rifle use and operation. Again, this remains a *military* manual. It exists as such because the Islamists remain at *war* and are not necessarily affecting a grievance (as would be the case for anyone sponsoring a professional hit on a particular individual). The Islamists *may* target an individual from time to time, but their "death wish list" remains exceedingly long and quite indiscriminate in application. That is, the jihadists target entire groups – Jews, Christians, apostates, etc.

> *"The target is on his way to work via public transportation. The moment he crosses the street to get to the best stop or to the main thoroughfare, the assassins, "two people" riding a motorcycle, open fire on the target and get away quickly in the opposite direction of the traffic."*

This technique appears to be a staple of the Middle East and of Hollywood. In reality, it remains more of a gang style hit than a professional assassination. True, the target is assassinated, but consider the events. First, the target is basically sprayed with bullets. These might hit innocent bystanders or, possibly, not produce sufficient injuries to warrant death. Remember, the human body possesses only a few lethal areas. Second, moving targets are extremely hard to hit even for accomplished shooters. This scenario possesses *two* motions – that of the victim (who could decide to run instead remain being hit while walking) and the moving shooter aboard a motorcycle. Lastly, the assassins dash off into "the opposite direction of the traffic." People, even in the chaotic Third World, tend to observe things going the wrong way. The last thing that a professional assassin wants is *recognition*. And what of the driver? Is he or she reliable and trustworthy?

> *"The target goes to work in his own automobile, which comes to get him in the morning and brings him back after work is over. A driver operates the car and the target's bodyguard sits beside the driver. The group of assassins, composed of three or four people, wait for the target's car. The waiting place should allow the assassin's car freedom of movement at any time. The assassin's car departs upon sighting the target's car and proceeds slowly until it comes to a spot which would allow it to block the way in front of the target's car. It then immediately stops, blocking the target's car. At the instant the assassin's car stops, the personnel in charge of killing or kidnapping the target get out, kill the bodyguard and the driver, and then execute their mission. This operation requires the utmost speed within a short*

time to avoid anyone pursuing the assassin's car or seeing any of the brothers."

This operation describes not an assassination, but an ambush reminiscent of what one would expect within a war zone. Several problems come immediate to mind. First, there is no set assassination environment; the entire operation rests upon stopping the victim's car at a point where the assassin's car can maneuver about. Any number of variables can serve to disrupt the final ambush site. Secondly, this type of operation requires extensive planning and coordination for which the "assassins" will not be able to practice anywhere near the actual ambush site. Third, witnesses are going to observe war going on in the neighborhood, particularly one that leaves two dead bodies lying around if not the third. Finally, supporting three or four assassins is going to involve a lot more people within the security perimeter necessitating a counterintelligence operation at the minimum. This assassination scenario opens too many aspects for future scrutiny and, certainly, at least "one" individual will eventually be caught for interrogation.

"Explosives are believed to be the safest weapon for the Mujahedeen. Using explosives allows them to get away from enemy personnel and to avoid being arrested. An assassination using explosives does not leave any evidence or traces at the operation site. In addition, explosives strike the enemy with sheer terror and fright."

Explosives may instill terror and fear, but they *do* leave much forensic evidence behind. Furthermore, the only sure way of permitting the assassins to escape the scene undetected remains to remote- or time-detonate the bomb ensuring that innocent parties may be affected. Because the "Mujahedeen" are more interested in killing their victim at any cost, they do not care about collateral damage. This eventually works against them as a resilient and knowledgeable forensics team will be able to track down parties associated with the bombing and, eventually, intelligence personnel will place the pieces together. Remember, the Israeli hit in Nicosia, Cyprus was eventually disclosed. All that it takes is time and the professional assassin bears little time to continuously keep looking over his or her shoulders.

> *"The substance Ricin, an extract from Castor Beans, is considered one of the most deadly poisons, .035 milligrams is enough to kill someone by inhaling or by injecting in a vein. However, though considered less poisonous if taken through the digestive system, chewing some Castor Beans could be fatal. It is a simple operation to extract Ricin, and Castor Beans themselves can be obtained from nurseries through the country."*

After discussing the merits of booby-traps and other fascinations with explosive devices, the al-Qaeda manual *finally* turns to techniques paralleling that employed by the professional assassin. Biological and chemical warfare turn a new chapter in killing, but this prospect does allow the assassin to focus on a particular individual and leave little evidence as to the precise nature of the assassination. Ricin poisoning offers symptoms similar to many other illnesses – vomiting, diarrhea, confusion, blueness of skin, etc. that, more than anything else, buys time for the assassin to escape. Unless the assassin bears a particularly strong fondness for keeping Castor Beans around him or her, there remains little to connect an individual to the crime.

The al-Qaeda manual moves into discussing Abrin (an herbal poison similar to Ricin and extracted from Precatory Beans) and certain "Frog poisons" that can be mixed with Nitrobenzene "cream" and which would kill a person within 15 minutes to an hour after mere touching. The manual becomes quite elaborate on the methods with which this slow but relentless poison mixture can be used to terminate an individual, making the concoction nearly ideal for the professional assassin. For those without access to, say, veterinarian supplies, the author(s) of the al-Qaeda document discuss how to employ the chemicals from spoiled foods to kill their victim. Part of this process, unnervingly, involves placing "about two spoonfuls of fresh excrement" into the food. Human feces remains one of the deadliest forces that can corrupt human health and can lead to death within a few hours after eating.

The al-Qaeda manual, after discussing a "non-Islamic" case of an insane individual perishing after eating human feces, completes with a discussion of interrogation and torture, which remains outside the subject matter of this book. The "Manchester Manual", in its entirety, represents a manual for war that assassinations merely represent a small part of the whole. Other al-Qaeda-related documents, however, shed further light on the organization's view of assassination. Al-Qaeda requires its assassins to be convinced that their actions are legitimate, maintain high levels of physical and combat effectiveness, master all weapons potentially used in assassination, bear a quick and responsive mind, display high levels of security awareness, be brave and steady, and possess a warrior mentality.[49] These remain common sense characteristics that most definitely apply to the professional assassin.

Al-Qaeda also considers seven "phases" of assassin: target designation, intelligence collection, method, planning, rehearsal, execution, and withdrawal.[50] The intelligence aspects of the operation are discussed most in depth and bear an appreciation of all aspects of the mission. This is appropriate

---

[49] Norman Cigar trans. *Al-Qa'ida's Doctrine for Insurgency: 'Abd Al-'Aziz Al-Muqrin's A Practical Course for Guerrilla War* (Washington: Potomac Books, 2009), 142.
[50] Ibid., 142-144.

for the lone assassin that has to endure widespread and difficult assignments without support or backup. Like the professional assassin, the al-Qaeda variety (more hit squads than lone operatives) remains conscious of operational security and how to subvert the target's own security apparatus.

This latter aspect remains critical, for almost anyone under the sights of an assassination sponsor undoubtedly bears a private security detail of some form or another. Few targets worth killing fall outside such a scope. Angered spouses and retaliatory family members probably resort to gang-style hits than employ professional assassins. At a minimum, the spontaneous murderer-in-law probably does not bear the knowledge and wherewithal to locate and employ a professional assassin without outside support (which would, undoubtedly, compromise their own security against incarceration).

Both the CIA and al-Qaeda approaches to targeted killing bear more identity with guerrilla operations than could be expected from the professional killer. While some common sense aspects are shared, the fundamental goal of Agency and al-Qaeda hits appears to be associated with change in governments, something that a professional assassin could never produce even if they succeeded in taking down a national leader (most nations possess ascendancy provisions).

9

CONCLUSION.

This book began with a question and that was, "why" even write a book about professional assassins? Of what value does learning about one of the most lethal human individuals possess? People die all of the time and many individuals literally get away with murder. Just consider, for instance, the ratio of Hollywood celebrities charged with murder against those actually *convicted* of murder. So why, therefore, single out a specific group of which the world really understands so little about? Part of the question can be answered by simply invoking security matters: we study so that we understand and we understand so that we need not fear.

A second question, not previously asked but of no doubt concerning to the reader, is "how" can we understand a secretive, extremely criminal, and exceptional exclusive individual? This answer remains a bit more complex and

101

subjective. In the intelligence field, for instance, answers are not readily known to the analyst. There is no such thing as the proverbial "declare all" document that, once captured, will inform a nation of the enemy's plans, intentions, and capabilities. On the contrary, the simplest desires may reveal themselves only after several months of painstaking investigation, conjecture, and reliance upon personal experience and knowledge.

Often, an intelligence analyst must weigh conflicting reports, decipher rumors, and formulate "best guess" estimates forged from very limited and undisclosed sources. Often times, a mere word is uttered barely within earshot that leads to prolonged research and investigation. Only after consolidating multiple sources from the academic to the archaic, from the familiar to the fantastical, can an individual even hope to piece together some semblance of the truth. Such remains the case with this particular book.

This effort began, quite innocently, nearly forty-five years ago when a fascination with things both military and political began and encompasses a life's work in studying guerrilla warfare, transnational criminal organizations (TCO), religious and political terrorism, and other low-intensity conflicts. It flourishes from chance meetings with some highly questionable characters and lifelong associations with the best that humanity has to offer. It rises from both formal academic study and informal personal inquisitiveness. And what you read here remains a mere tip of nature's darkest iceberg.

For someone dedicated to protecting the "dignity and integrity of innocent human life", *any* death sits heavily on the soul. If "just war" doctrine serves as any guide, the following should be the qualifications for imposing death upon another living soul:

✓ The damage inflicted by the targeted individual must

102

have been lasting, grave, and certain;

- ✓ All other means of ceasing the targeted individual's actions must have been shown to be impractical or ineffective;

- ✓ There must be serious prospects of success following the death of the target individual;

- ✓ The execution of a literal death sentence against the target individual must not produce evils and disorders greater than that committed by the individual to be killed.[51]

It remains debatable whether any assassin's target truly meets these requirements. Certainly, there are individuals around the world that the majority of people could make a logical claim for receiving a death sentence. Yet, precisely, *who* can make such a determination? Can the United States Government, who targeted citizen Anwar al-Awlaki with a Predator drone attack and yet permits his protégé, Fort Hood mass murderer Nidal Malik Hasan, confuse the judicial system by charging the latter with committing "work place violence", represent an impartial jury regarding the matter?

Wars are often debated long after hostilities cease with the victor(s) largely determining what was permissible or not. Few bother to avenge the death of an individual after he or she has been killed and this may, perhaps, offer on solution to the professional assassin equation. Nevertheless, in civilized society, no one person or organization can remain judge, jury, and executioner. If we succumb to the notion that a select few can determine the rights of the many, then where does it stop? Does a president, or a monarch, or even an activist judge rule more powerful than the "life, liberty, and pursuit of happiness"

---

[51] Paraphrased from *Catechism*, Paragraph #2309.

that all individual humans desire?

The professional assassin, therefore, probably reigns near the apex of human honesty. He or she kills for pay, and selects those singular individuals they can murder without losing sleep over the crime. Unlike soldiers who kill for the patriotism they often overlook during periods of peace or the national leader who orders killing for any number of reasons for which he or she may never feel threatened from, the assassin kills to pay the bills and experience the lifestyle that he or she desires.

Street criminals and narco-terrorists kill because of group mentality and the needs of authority. Islamic jihadists kill because they feel threatened by a world not of their choosing and believe that God ordains them to correct the situation. Thousands of lesser named individuals kill because of hatred, jealousy, revenge, power, or profit. Finally, a few rare – thank God – individuals kill simply because torturing animals no longer quenches their thirst for destruction. They kill because killing holds no special meaning for them other than it satisfies their warped concept of existence.

Is the professional assassin, then, a *murderer*? Absolutely! The Culture of Death within America where, for instance, 45+ *million* fetuses with aspirations to become human individuals (what *else* could they become?) have been killed simply because of the personal inconveniences they bring upon their mothers, has desensitized an entire culture to the prospects of death. Death is glorified within music. Death is glorified within the movies. Death is even *rewarded* within video games – you score more points and reach higher levels with killing various humans and other creatures.

In fact, the reason that you are reading this book on assassins is because *most* of the books out there are written about *the Assassins* and half of those books seem to discuss the game where killing represents the 'way' to winning. Yes, of course, there remains the occasional "good guy" who sweeps in saving the day – by *killing* off the bad guys. You would think that with all this fascination of killing, that professional assassin would rank amongst the top of any Internet list of desirable professions. Naturally, even the most moronic of individuals understands that 1.) Being an assassin represents a completely felonious way of life, and. 2.) Ninety-nine percent of the planet would last about five seconds serving as an assassin. The rest might make it to the sixth second.

This extraordinary – if not civilized – profession survives because there *are* individuals that can kill without being killed or apprehended. They have learned a trade which even the most decorated special operations soldier cannot endure (Spec Ops soldiers follow orders, operate under the auspices of a federal government, and are backed by echelons of military support personnel). The professional assassin represents *an individual.*

Perhaps this last element explains why they are so feared and distrusted amongst the rest of the world. Even gangsters and mafia members are often lauded for the "code" they follow. Some code; they just murder people who play the game. In the 1986 movie *Tough Guys* starring Kirk Douglas and Burt Lancaster, hired killer Leon B. Little (played by Eli Wallach) confronts Douglas and Lancaster's characters as they emerge from prison after 30 years announcing that he is under contract to kill them from *before* they were sent away. Such represents the tenacity of the professional assassin, but "Leon B. Little" still represents a character designed primarily for entertainment.

Real-life assassins never announce themselves to their victims. Nor do they show up with a double-barrel shotgun and attempt to proudly announce their occupation to the press. Perhaps this explains the decided lack of books on the trade.

Everything available is either an autobiography of someone employed within the services of a large (typically criminal) gang or an encyclopedic recitation of killers who murdered presidents, kings, and archdukes. In a sanitized world of desensitized wannabes, perhaps like the "mercenary soldier" of old (not to be confused with today's private military corporation employees), the assassin field will slowly fade out under the duress of some bureaucratized institution that heralds its killing as some form of environmental protection function.

Nevertheless, *somewhere* a prominent individual will find an untimely demise and newspapers around the planet will remark about how "unfortunate" it was that he died because of a "freak accident" or "drowning" or the result of a "strange set of mechanical failures". The local police will scratch their heads and sign off on the incident as something they would not wish to happen to them. If the newspaper or television journalist covers the "accident", it will likely be only because Miss Implants the latest starlet in Hollywood has already been arraigned and sentenced to community service for something most of us would receive at least a year in the slammer for. Hollywood, as always, will push the limits of gratuitous violence that is becoming rather comical with the "advancement" of computer-generated imagery.

Despite all of this, there will be at least *one* person whose primal honesty leads to a singular conclusion. We could tell you more, but then we would have to...

ABOUT THE AUTHOR

R.J. Godlewski (GOD LESS KEY) is an independent counterterrorism consultant, the director of the private International Nuclear Emergency Response Team [INERT], and the author of several novels, commentaries, and professional articles. He is the author and architect of the Web-based *Independent Counterterrorist* training program. He is currently a graduate student at American Military University completing his M.A. in Military Studies, Asymmetrical Warfare concentration, and graduate certificate in Security Management. Mr. Godlewski holds a B.A. in Intelligence Studies, Terrorism Studies concentration with a minor degree in Area Studies – Middle East with honors from American Military University. He further holds an undergraduate certificate in Explosive Ordnance Disposal and is a veteran of both the United States Navy and Navy Reserve. His most recent article is "Financial Counterintelligence: Fractioning the Lifeblood of Asymmetrical Warfare" *American Intelligence Journal* 29 no. 2 (2011): 24-33.